MAKING TRADITIONAL TEDDY BEARS

MAKING
TRADITIONAL
TEDDY BEARS

BRIAN AND DONNA GIBBS

David & Charles

A DAVID & CHARLES BOOK

First published in the UK in 1997
Reprinted 1997, 1998

ISBN 0 7153 0431 3
Photography by Tim Hill
Styling by Zöe Hill
Book design by Hammond Hammond

Printed in Italy by LEGO SpA
for David & Charles
Brunel House   Newton Abbot   Devon

CONTENTS

MAKING A TRADITIONAL TEDDY BEAR

BRING ON THE BEARS

INTRODUCTION

For nearly a century the teddy bear has been one of the most popular and comforting toys ever created. Over the years the teddy has evolved and progressed from a simple child's toy to the present day collectors item giving pleasure to their owners both young and old. As the traditional teddy bear has now become so popular and, unfortunately in many cases very expensive, the demand for patterns and information to make teddy bears has greatly increased. As a result this book has been written to enable anyone to make their own collector's quality traditional teddy bear that is fully jointed and has all the charm and character of the teddy bear as it should be. Many of the traditional skills and techniques have been incorporated into the 12 designs in this book to ensure your bear will look and be as well-loved as the teddy bear of yesteryear. You may find, as countless others have, that making teddy bears can be an addictive and rewarding hobby as you are re-creating the nostalgia and pleasure of childhood bears by using traditional methods and materials. Using the patterns in this book, your finished creations will become the heirlooms of your family and make a fine addition to any bear collector's hug.

Even if you have never made a teddy bear or soft toy before, the step-by-step instructions are written clearly to help everyone to make their chosen bears. There are also countless tricks of the trade, clear diagrams and photographs to help you achieve a teddy bear to be proud of. Also included are sections on the history of the teddy bear and a comprehensive section that will explain all of the currently available materials and components necessary in making traditional jointed teddy bears. This book will be invaluable for both beginner and expert alike as there are many tips and techniques clearly and simply explained in the comprehensive step by step section. This is followed by the pattern selection that will take you through every one of the bears featured in the book. If as well as making teddy bears you have an old teddy that is in need of a little tender loving care then the bear clinic section will help to guide you in restoring him to his original glory. Finally, listed at the back of the book, you will find a suppliers list of materials so that wherever you are in the world, you too will be able to obtain the same quality of materials as used in this book to make your own traditional teddy bears.

HISTORY OF THE TEDDY BEAR

The first teddy bears are thought to have been made around the year 1902, with two manufacturers both claiming to be the originators – though neither of them is able to support their claim with conclusive documentary evidence. However, it is generally accepted that the 'Teddy Bear' originated as a result of a cartoon by Clifford Berryman entitled 'Drawing the line in Mississippi' that appeared in a Washington newspaper in November 1902. It showed President Theodore (Teddy) Roosevelt refusing to shoot a captive bear cub during a bear hunt arranged for his benefit while he was on a visit to Mississippi. A Russian immigrant named Morris Michtom who was the proprietor of a small store in Brooklyn that sold sweets, novelties and toys, many of the latter handmade by himself and his wife Rose, saw the cartoon and immediately conceived the idea of re-creating the image as a toy bear cub made from a soft brown plush and with moveable arms and legs.

The prototype was displayed in the store window alongside a newspaper clipping of the original cartoon and aroused considerable interest, so Michtom decided he would like to market the idea. He wrote to the President, asking permission to market the toy and call it 'Teddy's Bear', and was extremely surprised to receive an answer in the President's own hand which read, 'I don't think my name is worth much to the toy bear cub business, but you are welcome to use it.' Michtom then made samples of the bear and sent one to the President

With care you can make modern bears with the same style and charm as these genuine antiques.

and another to the buyer of Butler Brothers, a large toy wholesaler. In 1903 Butler Brothers decided to take the entire output of these teddy bears and guaranteed credit with the suppliers of the plush fabric needed to manufacture them. This was the beginning of the Ideal Novelty & Toy Co., which in 1938 was renamed the Ideal Toy Co. If the original letter from the President granting permission could ever be produced, this would establish the claim by the Michtom family beyond all doubt.

However, the other claim to the title of creator of the teddy bear is from the German toy manufacturer Margarete Steiff, who already owned a well-established company making felt toys and exporting them all over the world. These toys, exceedingly popular at the time, were mainly domestic and farm animals including cats, dogs, pigs and horses, but no bears. In 1902, Margarete Steiff's nephew Richard, an art student, made several visits to the zoo at Stuttgart, during which he sketched a large number of the animals at the zoo – including bears. Thus the idea came to him that perhaps he could design a toy bear that would be more cuddly and realistic than the felt animals that his aunt was currently producing.

Richard proved to be a very competent designer, producing a jointed teddy bear with moveable head and limbs and a fluffy mohair finish. Although Margarete was unenthusiastic about the toy she allowed it to be sent to America in an attempt to market it, but was not at all surprised that it was not accepted by any of the agents and that no orders were received. Undaunted, Richard went with his brothers to a toy fair in Leipzig in 1903, taking his bear along, but it was not given prominence and its creator naturally felt rather dejected at this apparent lack of interest in his design. However, on the last day as the fair was drawing to a close and all the exhibits were being packed away, things took a turn for the better for Richard when he was approached by Hermann Berg from the New York wholesalers Geo. Borgfeldt & Co. Berg told Richard that he thought the fair rather dull and was uninspired by all the usual felt toys as he was looking for something soft and cuddly. Hardly able to believe the opportunity that had presented itself to him at the very last minute, Richard produced his bear – and Berg was absolutely delighted. It was exactly what he was looking for, and he was so impressed that an order was placed almost immediately for 3000 bears. On hearing the good news, Margarete rather reluctantly agreed that the design was obviously acceptable, only to have her doubts removed when a second order for another 3000 bears was received.

At this point, the story takes on a rather fanciful turn with no certain way of substantiating the facts. It is claimed that at Alice Roosevelt's wedding in 1906 the Steiff company provided teddy bears to adorn the tables at the reception – and when one of the guests asked to which species these bears belonged, the President is alleged to have replied that they were a new species called 'Teddy' bears. As with the first story there is no proof to settle the matter conclusively, but the main fact is that the teddy did evolve and went on to become immensely popular. Production from the two companies increased at a phenomenal rate, with the Steiff factory expanding three times between 1903 to 1908.

Around this time the teddy bear industry began to develop elsewhere, with the English company J. K. Farnell Co., manufacturers of tea cosies and pin cushions, also entering the field. After the death of Margarete Steiff in May 1909 her company continued to expand, opening warehouses in New York, Sydney and several European countries. Other German bear manufacturers appeared just before the First World War, but their production of teddy bears was cut short as the factories and their employees were used for war work. This helped to

boost the teddy bear industry in England, where Deans and Chad Valley produced their first jointed mohair teddy bears. The popularity of teddy bears was further galvanized with the introduction in 1920 of the Rupert Bear comic strip character in the *Daily Express*, which gave rise to various Rupert merchandise now eagerly sought after by avid collectors.

A ban on toy imports from Germany during the 1920s and 1930s further enhanced the British teddy bear market, and it was during this period that Chiltern, another household name in teddy bears, and the Merrythought Co. in Ironbridge, Shropshire, were founded, in 1923 and 1930 respectively. War again intervened in 1939 and as raw materials were in very short supply bears were designed with shorter limbs and muzzles and alternative fabrics.

Eventually the industry started to recover worldwide and in the 1950s the teddy bear underwent a further change, with the introduction of synthetic fabrics, safety eyes and manmade alternatives such as vinyl noses which helped to cut down on material costs and speed up production. Fully washable teddy bears filled with foam chips then started to appear, and eventually the teddy in later years evolved as a one-piece unit, completely unjointed. This loss of character eventually proved to be unpopular and the traditional teddy that was becoming so difficult to obtain started to reappear when it became obvious to the larger manufacturers that the teddy bear was starting to become a collectors' item as well as a child's toy. The major manufacturers quickly capitalized on this growing trend and started issuing classic reproductions of their earlier designs, using traditional materials. These bears were more expensive, especially those that were of limited production, which added to their interest for the collector. Nowadays, their value as collectables has significantly increased their availability and there is a growth in the number of craftspeople who specialize in making traditional and very limited edition teddy bears. These people, generally known as 'teddy bear artists', often sell their work via the many teddy bear trade shows and conventions all over the world. Their contribution to the industry has been of great value in increasing the popularity of the teddy bear which evolved so many years before as a simple child's toy.

MATERIALS

There is a large variety of materials available for teddy-bear making, ranging from the traditional mohair in various qualities to synthetic fabrics. Your choice is a wide one and you should find no difficulty in obtaining your materials, either from a shop or from one of the specialist mail order companies (see page 126). The latter will send small samples on request so that you can examine the fabric before purchasing, although you should be prepared to pay a small charge for this service. Many teddy bear suppliers only sell their fabrics in full, half and quarter yards (or metres), so the amount of fabric given for the bears in this book can sometimes be a little on the generous side.

Whichever type of material you decide upon the rule is to try to buy the best, especially if your bear is intended to become a collector's item or family heirloom. If you are making it for a small child, make sure that the fabric complies with the approved safety standards.

Each pattern in this book gives the qualities and types of the mohair or fur fabrics used for the bears

illustrated to enable you to replicate them as accurately as possible. However, you may decide to change the types of materials or pile lengths to suit your taste or pocket – the bear will obviously look different, but beauty is in the eye of the beholder and you may feel that your version is an improvement!

MOHAIR

This is a natural material derived from the fleece of the angora goat, thought to have been first discovered in 1550 at Angora in Turkey (now Ankara). It was not readily available in Europe until the early 19th century, when it became popular for use in textiles. This natural straight fibre was hard-wearing, took dye easily and, because of its non-shiny appearance, made a very realistic fur as well, which was a bonus to teddy-bear makers. As a consequence, mohair has for many years been the material used for the vast majority of traditional teddy bears sold by bear artists and leading collectors' bear manufacturers alike.

1   2   3   4

Mohair is woven on to a backing, usually of cotton, which is ideal in that it will not stretch out of shape when the finished bear is stuffed. It is relatively expensive, as the fleece is not in such plentiful supply as sheep's wool and the various complex stages of weaving, dying and finishing can often take up to eight weeks to complete. However, fortunately for teddy-bear makers, mohair is quite easy to obtain and is manufactured in more than one country in all the traditional teddy-bear golds and browns, as well as a vast array of other colours.

Mohair is sold in a variety of qualities which dictate the pile length and the finish applied to it. The pile length can be from around ⅛ to 1 inch (4mm to 25mm) or more and is measured from the tip down to the backing on the pile side; the longer the pile, the more expensive the fabric.

A range of finishes can be applied to the mohair pile. The most basic is ordinary straight pile, which will be exactly as it states – straight! This is usually very effective on the shorter pile lengths of ⅛ inch (4mm) or so for making miniature bears. Next there is the distressed pile, which is the most popular because the finish gives the appearance of an old bear that has seen plenty of use. The effect is created by a steaming process that gives a random swirl effect to the pile. A variant of this is curly pile, which has a generally uniform effect rather than the random look of the distressed.

Another popular fabric is sparse mohair, in which the pile density is reduced so that the backing shows through the pile quite easily. It also sometimes has a slight distress to it. This is a good choice if you want to create a very old-looking teddy bear that gives the impression of having been well-loved and cuddled over many years. Also available is tipped mohair, which has a usually fairly long pile of a uniform base colour with the addition of a contrasting colour at the tip of the pile. This creates a frosted appearance which gives an attractive effect to the finished bear – but remember that if the bear is to have a shaved muzzle there will be a colour change when the pile is trimmed.

These are the main types of mohair, although there may be subtle differences according to the

1. *Distressed mohair*
2. *German mohair*
3. *Sparse-pile mohair*
4. *Tipped mohair*
5. *Mini-bear mohair*
6. *Straight pile mohair*
7. *Fur fabric*
8. *Velvet*

5   6   7   8

country in which they are produced. There are also variations such as mohair/cotton and mohair/silk mixes, both of which are very useful for particular textures and specific effects. You will find that the majority of specialist suppliers will be quite happy to give you advice on what will suit your needs and budget.

ALPACA PLUSH

This is a natural fabric of the same quality as mohair, manufactured in a similar way but from the wool of a species of South American llama. It is used in exactly the same way as mohair but is not quite so easily obtainable.

SYNTHETIC FUR FABRICS

These are made in a far greater choice of colour and will probably be available virtually anywhere at a relatively low cost. They are made with two main types of backing. The more expensive will have a woven type which, like the mohair fabric, will resist stretch and allow you to make a firm bear. The cheaper types will invariably have a knitted or jersey back. They can still be used to good effect but allowance must be made for stretch and so for best results the bear must not be over-stuffed. If this fabric is all you can obtain, or you want to make your first bear using a cheaper fabric to see the finished result, you could consider making the backing more stable by ironing on fusible interfacing as used in dressmaking. This is available in various weights, so experiment first on a scrap of the selected fur fabric to find the weight you need. As these synthetic fabrics have a melting point, you must also test the iron temperature – start at the lowest available and adjust it as necessary.

The piles on synthetic fur fabric can vary greatly in quality and the more expensive woven-backed fabrics will naturally have a denser pile. When selecting your fabric, smooth the pile in various directions to see if it resists matting. The best way of doing this is to apply slight pressure in a circular motion with your forefinger or thumb and then smooth the pile back in the original direction. If the pile has started to matt already the fabric is best rejected as the finished bear will soon begin to look rather shabby. You should also avoid any fabrics that shed pile easily; this can be ascertained by gently tugging the fibres at the centre of a small sample away from the cut edges.

OTHER BODY FABRICS

Not all teddy bears are best made from fur. Many benefit from being made from velvet, which is a very fine and soft material with a short pile that stands straight up. It is available in many colours. Another variant is Dralon, an acrylic fibre. Indeed, there is such a large assortment of fabrics available these days that the range is virtually unlimited – we have seen patchwork teddies, calico teddies embroidered for added interest and even tartan print. The choice is yours!

FELT

Although you can use suedette, velvet, suede or leather on the paws of teddies, the traditional material to use is felt. This is available in a variety of colours and should be easy to obtain in a shade to match your chosen teddy fur. Felt is made by milling wet fibres until they are interlocked and matted and then applying pressure to them. It is available in a variety of qualities, the cheapest being acrylic felt, although this is best avoided as it tends to be rather thin. A 60/40 wool/synthetic mix is a good choice for durability and reasonable cost but best of all is pure wool felt, which is obviously much thicker and has a finer texture. It is more expensive but, as with all felts, there is no grain so any cutting out can be accomplished with the minimum of waste.

THREADS

TACKING THREAD This is a soft, slightly fluffy thread, most commonly used in white so that it shows up well. It is used for securing the fabric pieces in position after they have been pinned together. This allows you to remove the pins to make stitching the seams much easier, after which the tacking thread is simply pulled out.

POLYESTER/COTTON SEWING THREAD This is a general-purpose thread which combines strength with durability and is suitable for use in a sewing machine. It is available in a wide range of colours and you should choose one which as nearly as possible matches the backing of the fabric which your bear is to be made from.

STRONG OR FINISHING THREAD This thread is easily identified from ordinary sewing thread by its heavier and thicker texture. It is used for closing the final seams of a bear such as back openings, for attaching glass eyes and for making thread joints for very tiny bears. The strength of this thread is very important and ideally you should not be able to break it with your hands; look for a mix of 75 per cent polyester to 25 per cent cotton or 100 per cent polyester to give the added strength. If you intend to hand sew the complete bear it is best to use the strong thread throughout for added strength to the seams.

NOSE THREAD This is used for embroidering bears' noses and also for stitching claws on to the paws. The thread to look for is Perle, which is normally used for embroidery; it is very suitable for teddy bears as it is often mercerized to make it soft and lustrous. It comes in a wide selection of colours and although black is the general colour used for noses some teddies look equally grand with one of the browner shades, depending of course on the colour of your chosen fabric. It is available as thick or thin thread, the latter being especially suitable for stitching the noses of the miniature bears.

FILLINGS

WOOD WOOL Many years ago, the most commonly used filling for teddy bears was wood wool (under the trade name 'Excelsior'). This is extremely thin, finely shredded wood closely resembling straw. In its day wood wool was easily available as it was widely used for packing delicate items such as china and glass. However, these days the trend is for plastic chips and these are certainly of no use for filling teddy bears!

Wood wool is not suitable for children's bears as it is not washable and may have a high dust content, but those who wish to make a collector's bear will find that it is still available from some specialist suppliers of teddy bear materials. It is often sold semi-compressed, in which case it will need to be placed in a large box and teased apart before use. Before buying, try to obtain a small sample first as some qualities of modern wood wool can be a little coarse.

POLYESTER This is by far the most commonly available filling, and the easiest to use. It is especially suitable for children's bears. There are various qualities and grades to choose from, the bottom of the range being the coloured cotton waste and the top the hi-loft varieties. The cheaper grades are thin and dense, while the better quality hollow-fibre ones are fluffier. For teddy bears the hi-loft is best as it allows you to obtain a firm yet even filling to your bear and will not compact down into lumps as the cheaper varieties may do.

KAPOK This is a vegetable fibre and is still often used in the upholstery business. It has a very silky feel but the fine fibres tend to detach themselves and float around, so if you do use it in large quantities it is best to wear a small dust mask for safety. It is ideal for miniature teddy bears and is delightfully easy to use, but it is not really suitable for the larger bears as it would make them very heavy.

PELLETS There is a trend these days to use plastic pellets as a part filling to give character and 'sag' to the finished bear. These small, rounded pieces of plastic (rather similar to rice) give a very stable, heavy bear. Do not confuse them with bean bag filling, which is extremely light polystyrene beads and is not suitable for bear-making.

JOINTS

Joints are a very important feature for the traditional teddy. Very early bears would have had stout cardboard joints. These days, the two main types of joint available are wooden or plastic and which to use is a matter of choice unless your bear

is intended for a child, in which case you should use the plastic type for safety reasons.

Wooden joints comprise two wooden discs, two metal washers and a split pin or cotter pin. The advantages of wooden joints are that they can be adjusted as explained on page 29 and they tend to be more durable (and usually cheaper) than plastic joints. However, to assemble them correctly you will need to purchase a pair of slim-nosed pliers. It is also possible to buy wooden joints with a nyloc nut and bolt replacing the split pin but these tend to be hard to find in a variety of sizes and a spanner is needed to secure them. An easier method of securing bolt joints using two nuts is described in full in the instructions for making Harvey bear on page 118.

Plastic joints are composed of two plastic discs, one with a moulded shank attached and a one-way fixing washer of metal or plastic that, once fitted, cannot be removed without destroying the joint, so you must be sure that your joint is correctly positioned before the final fixing.

With the exception of Grizzler, the teddy bears in this book use the same size for all five joints. You may occasionally see other designs giving one size of joint for the legs, another for the arms and even a third size for the head. This is largely unnecessary in a standard teddy bear design and may add to the cost of the finished bear as the joints are often sold only in sets of five or ten.

EYES

BOOT-BUTTON EYES As these were used on the very early bears, they are the most popular choice for a traditional teddy. Boot-button eyes are exactly what you would expect – boot buttons! These were originally used because no commercially manufactured eyes were available at the time. Genuine boot buttons are still to be found occasionally but it is easier to find the modern reproductions.

GLASS EYES These were used from 1909 onwards and are today widely available from many specialist suppliers in a variety of colours and sizes, both with and without pupils. There are two main types supplied – the looped type that have a wire loop moulded into the glass at the back of the eye and need no further preparation, and the type supplied on a wire with an eye moulded at each end, requiring you to cut the wire and loop it. Buying

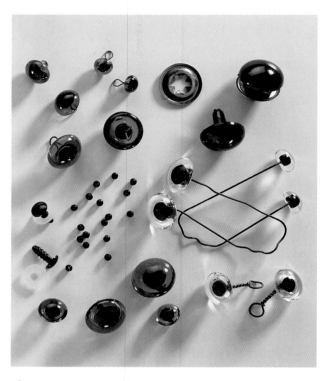

glass eyes on a single wire does not guarantee that you will have an exactly matching pair, so it pays to scrutinize them carefully before purchase.

PLASTIC SAFETY EYES These eyes are again widely available in a range of colours and sizes and are essential when making children's bears. They are one-piece moulded plastic with a shank and a one-way washer that is not removable once fitted and are therefore very safe for children.

BEADS Small glass or plastic beads can be used for miniature teddy bears and are sewn on through the hole in the bead.

VOICES

What traditional teddy bear would be complete without a voice? These are available in a selection of sizes and come in several forms from growlers down to a little squeak for the smaller bears. The growlers are usually in a cylindrical plastic case and have a bellows and weight operated by tipping the bear forwards or back depending on the way they are installed in the bear. Also available are little sealed music boxes that are pull-string or key-operated and produce popular tunes. These easily fitted accessories will add to the character of your finished teddy bear.

TOOLS & EQUIPMENT

Few tools are necessary to make teddy bears and those on the following list will probably have an everyday use in the home. However, one or two of them may be difficult to find, so we have suggested alternatives. Try to buy good-quality tools as poorly manufactured ones will always let you down and make each job more of a chore than a pleasure.

PATTERN-MAKING

You will need tracing paper to trace off the required pattern and some lightweight craft card to use for making your pattern templates (empty cereal boxes will make an ideal substitute). A fairly soft pencil is needed for tracing patterns and marking out the templates. Finally, a fine, felt tip permanent marker pen is ideal for marking the cutting lines on the back of your fabric along with any pattern information such as joint and eye positions.

GLUES

There are two types of glue that are useful for teddy bear-making: clear all-purpose craft glue (usually sold in tubes), which is ideal for gluing the nose templates into position before embroidering the noses, and white water-soluble p.v.a. glue, diluted with water in equal parts and used to reinforce the fabric edging on the smaller bears to prevent fraying. This glue is almost transparent when dry.

SEWING MACHINE

There is not a pattern in this book that cannot be completely sewn by hand but most people will wish to use a sewing machine and the step-by-step instructions have been written with this in mind. You do not need a special machine – a basic model will do the job just as well as the modern computerized machines and in fact many of the bears in this book were sewn using a very old but reliable Singer hand-operated sewing machine

dating from 1933! It is vitally important with all sewing machines to keep the mechanical parts clean and free from the fluff and fibres that accumulate when you are using fur fabrics and mohair, especially around the bobbin case. Try to get into the habit of inspecting these parts frequently and cleaning them when necessary. You will find this much easier if you loosen the fibres with a small, clean, dry paint brush while at the same time using a vacuum cleaner with a small nozzle attached to the hose. This will only take a couple of minutes but will ensure trouble-free sewing. It is very important with electric machines to disconnect the electricity supply before you attempt to clean any moving parts.

NEEDLES

If you are intending to use a sewing machine you will need a size 14 to 16 machine needle, either a ballpoint if you are using a knitted or jersey-backed fabric or a sharp or regular point needle if you will be sewing woven-backed material such as mohair and the better quality fur fabrics.

For tacking the pieces of your bear together (or handsewing), we recommend a size 5 to 7 needle, again either ballpoint or sharp depending on the type of fabric you will be sewing.

For finishing the seams, you will find that a longer needle is much easier for making secure and neat final seams. A long darning needle of approximately 2½ inches (65mm) in length and either size 5 or 7 will be most suitable.

For attaching glass eyes to a bear, a specialist 'doll makers' needle is needed. These relatively slender needles are approximately 5 inches (130mm) in length, and are essential to pass the thread through the completed head of the teddy bear.

Finally, another needle is required for embroidering the nose and claws of your bear –

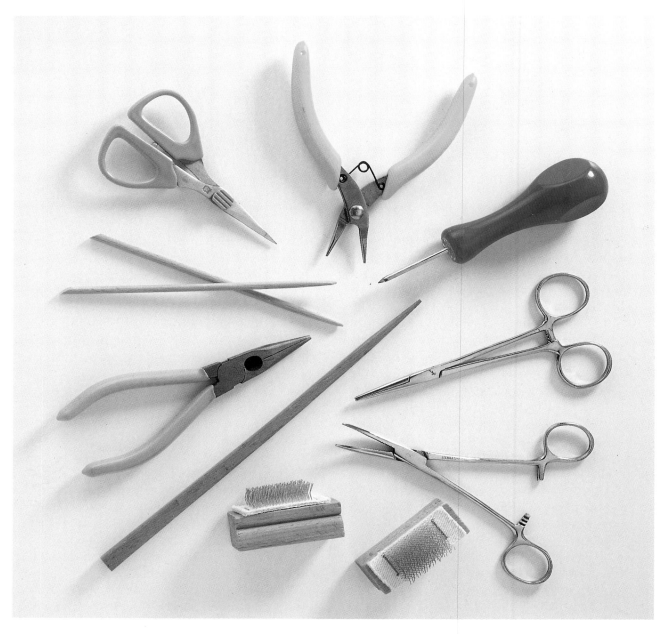

again a darning needle but of larger gauge to accommodate the thicker thread (size 14 should be ideal). For the miniature bears, when you will be using the thinner nose thread, a size 5 to 7 needle should be used. All needles should be sharp and in good condition.

THIMBLE

When you are sewing by hand you will find that the needle can become a little difficult to pass through the thicker, bulkier parts of the bear. To overcome this it is a good idea to purchase a leather thimble, which will also cushion your finger when you have

Useful tools: (clockwise from top left) *embroidery scissors, pliers, awl, two pairs of forceps, teazel brushes, a stuffing stick, pliers and two small stuffing sticks.*

a lot of pinning to do through bulky seams. Another benefit of a leather thimble is that you can wear it on your little finger, which will allow you to wrap the thread around your finger and pull tightly without the thread cutting into your skin.

PINS

All teddy bear-making will require the use of pins to position the various pieces securely prior to tacking and sewing. The best pins are the extra-long type as you will be using relatively thick fabric. They should also have coloured plastic or glass heads to aid visibility in dense fur. These pins are usually supplied on a plastic wheel, which serves two useful purposes: the pins are always neatly stored and, more importantly, they are replaced on the wheel after use, thus making absolutely sure that they are never mistakenly left inside a teddy bear.

SCISSORS
There are three types of scissors that are generally used for bear-making: craft scissors, fabric scissors and embroidery scissors. The craft scissors are ordinary (usually quite inexpensive) household scissors, needed for cutting out paper or card pattern pieces and templates. Fabric scissors will cost a little more as they need to be of good quality and sharp. However, as the majority of fabric pieces for bear-making are quite small, it is both impractical and expensive to purchase very large fabric scissors; a smaller pair of approximately 5 inches (130mm) will cut out the smallest pieces with ease and be light and comfortable to use.

A small pair of embroidery scissors will be needed to cut threads after sewing and also to trim away the fur on the teddy bear's nose prior to embroidering it. They are also ideal for cutting out the very small fabric pieces if you are making any of the miniature teddy bears.

PLIERS
If you will be using the traditional wooden joints in your teddy bear then a good pair of pliers are essential to turn down the legs of the split pins to secure the joints. They must be the slim, long-nosed type and of good quality. Try to purchase a pair of approximately 6 inches (150mm) in overall length with a wire-cutting facility. This will be useful to cut the wire on glass eyes. If you have difficulty obtaining such pliers a small pair of inexpensive wire or side cutters will also be needed – do not be tempted to cut the glass eye wires with scissors as you could quite easily ruin both the eyes and the scissors.

AWL
An awl, or bradawl, is a sharp-pointed tool available from most hardware stores. This will be used to make small holes in the card templates and in the fabric by parting the weave rather than cutting any of the threads. It is also an essential little tool for jointing the bears and for inserting the eyes. As you will find, teddy-bear fabric, particularly the woven-backed furs, can be quite tough so it is necessary to use an implement with a handle if possible, though a knitting needle will do instead if an awl is not to be found.

STUFFING STICKS
There are commercially manufactured stuffing sticks on the market but these are usually hard to obtain. Instead, you can use the handle of a wooden spoon. These are available in a variety of sizes and you will find that the bowl of the spoon fits very comfortably in the palm of your hand. Alternatively, you can make your own stuffing sticks from short lengths of ½ inch (12mm) diameter round wooden dowel with one end smoothed and shaped with sandpaper. For smaller areas, chopsticks are equally useful.

SAFETY TOOL
A safety tool is designed to aid the secure placement of the one-way washers used on the plastic joints and the safety eyes. As these washers are often metal, they can need quite a lot of force to push them on to the shank. A safety tool is a flat metal tool, usually aluminium, that has two holes drilled into it, one large and one small for use with various sizes of shanks. This tool is used to push the washer firmly and squarely home. An alternative is to use a cotton reel which, when placed over the washer and shank, can be lightly tapped with a small hammer to perform the same function.

TEASEL BRUSH
When the teddy bear is complete there will inevitably be pile trapped in the seams, but this is easily lifted with a teasel brush. These invaluable items are generally made from short wire bristles mounted on to a small wooden block. They are available from most haberdashery departments and specialist teddy-bear suppliers, but an alternative teasel brush can be found in pet shops, where they are sold as small grooming brushes. These are made in the same way as the conventional teasel brush but are a little larger and have a handle, making them more comfortable to use but rather more expensive.

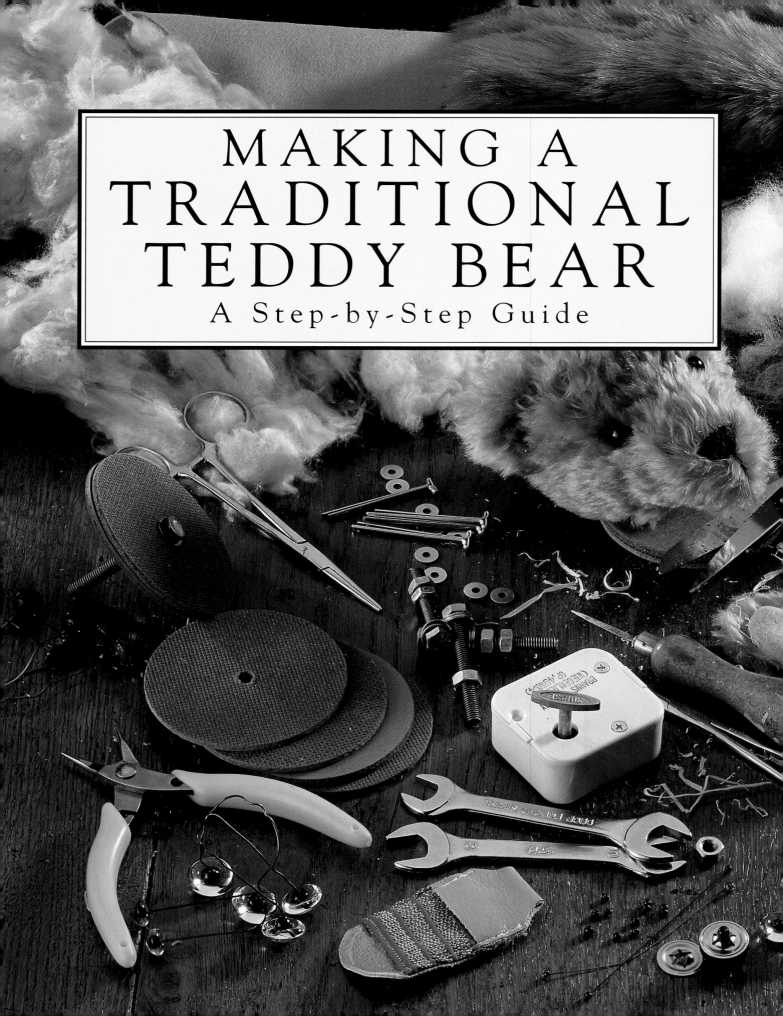

MAKING A
TRADITIONAL
TEDDY BEAR

A Step-by-Step Guide

Once you have decided which teddy bear you would like to make the first step is to make a copy of the pattern. If it requires enlarging, the easiest way to do this is to take the book along to your local photocopying shop and ask for a copy of the pattern enlarged by the percentage figure stated on the pattern. Even if the pattern does not require enlarging you may still wish to use a photocopy to save time as otherwise you will need to make a tracing of the pattern pieces from the book, transferring all of the information such as joint and opening positions, pile direction, whether the piece is to be cut from fur or felt and how many are required.

CARD TEMPLATES

When you have a copy of your pattern, the next step is to make a set of working card templates of the pattern pieces. To do this, paste the pattern copy directly on to thin card, using either a proprietary paper glue or one of the spray adhesives sold in art stores. The card will be available from the same source, sold as craft card, although you will find that empty cereal boxes will make an ideal substitute. When the glue has dried completely, cut out all of the templates using your general-purpose or craft scissors – not your good-quality scissors as cutting card and paper will take off the keen sharpness needed for cutting fabric. You will see that on the legs, for example, there are instructions to cut four with two reversed and, until you get into the swing of bear-making, a useful tip is to cut out all of the reverses and pairs from card so that you will end up with four card leg templates. This will avoid the common mistake of cutting out unequal pairs and reverses from your fabric and will also enable you to position the templates more economically on the fabric before marking.

You will see from the patterns that some of the pieces have joint positions and as these need to be marked on to the back of the fabric, you will need to make a small hole in the card at the appropriate points. It is a good idea to mark each piece with the pattern name and size of bear. This information will be helpful if you would like to make more than one bear from the same pattern. Another tip is to make a small hole with a paper punch at the top of each pattern piece so that the pieces can be strung together and kept safely until they are needed again. Card templates are quite durable and even if you

have used empty cereal packets you will find the templates will last for many bears.

MARKING FABRIC

Before marking any fabric, the first step is to identify the pile direction of your chosen fur. The pile may run from top to bottom or from edge to edge and the easiest way to establish the direction is to stroke the fur with the palm of your hand to find which way is smoothest. Mark the back of the fabric with an arrow, with the point of it following the smooth direction of the pile. This arrow will be an important guide to correct positioning of the templates when marking your fabric.

Marking out on the back of the fabric.

On some materials, particularly the distressed mohairs, the pile goes in different directions. The main pile direction is usually still detectable but each pattern piece should be checked carefully with particular importance given to the head sides and gusset to ensure that the pile is running in a satisfactory direction.

Lay the full set of card templates including all the reverses and pairs (but excluding of course those that will be cut from felt) on to the back of your fabric and position them roughly, matching the arrow directions on the templates to the arrow you have marked on the fabric backing. Adjust the spacing and placement of the templates to give you the most economic layout. When you are completely satisfied draw around each template in turn, using a fine permanent marker pen that leaves an easily visible line. It is essential that the pattern information on each template be transferred to the fabric, including joint and dart positions, pile direction and of course what each piece is. Do this as each individual piece is marked to avoid any confusion at a later stage. Also mark out any pieces that are to be cut from felt (these will not of course need a grain direction). When you have checked that all of the pieces are marked and identified, the templates can all be strung together and placed aside for future use.

CUTTING OUT

Lay your fabric fur side down on a clean, flat surface. It is very important that only the backing fabric is cut, not the actual pile, so you will need to slide the point of your fabric scissors between the pile to the level of the backing and then make small snipping cuts around the outlines of the pieces. This may sound time-consuming, but in fact it is quite easy and quick to do. Before cutting any fabric, remember that it is far better to check twice and cut once!

When you have cut out all the pieces it is worth spending a little time to pair them up where appropriate, making certain that you have cut out the correct number of arms, legs and so on. It is always worth keeping a little scrap material as this will be useful for setting the stitch length and tension on your sewing machine and for practising on when you reach the muzzle-trimming stage.

MAKING UP YOUR BEAR

With the exception of the miniature bears, all the designs in this book include a seam allowance of ¼ inch (7mm) within the pattern outlines and you should use a medium stitch length when sewing your seams.

MAKING THE ARMS

Start by making the arms. You will need one inner arm piece, the corresponding outer arm (which is the longer of the two) and one of the felt paw pads. Lay the paw pad on the pile of the inner arm with the straight edges level as shown in Fig.1 and pin together. Tuck in as much as possible of the fur as you go as this will ensure the finished seam is neat and tidy – you will find that a long pin or needle is the most useful tool for this purpose. The pad can

The correct cutting method.

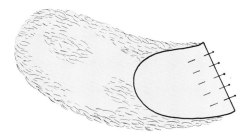

Fig.1 Pin the felt paw piece to the inner arm.

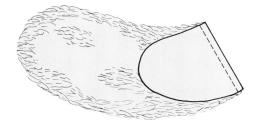

Fig.2 Tack the paw piece in place.

now be tacked in place, using tacking cotton of a contrasting colour to the sewing thread and taking fairly large but even running stitches along the seam line (Fig.2). (Tacking is essential to keep everything accurately held together and also makes sewing easier than it would be with pins in place.) Remove the pins, stitch the pad into position and then pull out the tacking thread. Finally, trim off all loose thread ends and your inner arm is now complete.

Open the arm out flat (Fig.3) and pin it to the outer arm right sides together, starting with a pin at the top of the arm and one at the paw tip to ensure the arm pieces are reasonably level. Continue

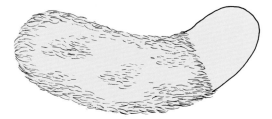

Fig.3 Open the completed inner arm out flat.

pinning around the remaining edges at intervals of approximately ½ inch (12mm), depending on the pile length of your particular fabric. Check that everything is in line and that all the edges are level and free from any puckers, adjusting if necessary by removing and reinserting the pins while smoothing the material to ease out any irregularities. Tack around the pinned arm and remove all of the pins, then, starting from the top of the marked opening, sew around the whole arm, terminating at the bottom of the marked opening and ensuring that the opening is free for turning and jointing. Make sure that all the material has been adequately caught in your seam and that the start and finish stitches at the seam opening are securely fastened before you pull out the tacking stitches.

Now turn the completed arm right side out through the seam opening. If you have any difficulty with the bulk of material you may find one of your stuffing sticks to be helpful here, especially on the arms of the smaller bears. Do not worry at this stage about any fur pile trapped in the seams as this will be dealt with later. Make the second arm in the same way, the only difference being that that it will be reversed to make a finished pair.

MAKING THE LEGS

Each leg is made by taking two leg pieces, one right and one left, and placing them right sides together, keeping the bottom straight edge level. Pin the two sides in place (Fig.4), using plenty of pins and leaving the straight edge open for the footpad, which will be pinned into position a little later. Check that the fabric is free from puckers and then tack the leg pieces together. Remove all of the pins

and stitch the leg pieces (Fig.5), remembering to leave the opening for turning and jointing as shown on the pattern and the bottom straight edge. Pull out all the tacking stitches and check that all the fabric is caught in the seam and that the stitches at the opening edges are securely fastened.

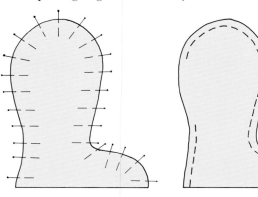

Fig.4 Pin the two leg pieces together, leaving the bottom edge open.

Fig.5 Stitch the leg pieces together, leaving the bottom edge open.

Fold the felt footpad in half lengthways and crease it slightly so that when you open it out you will be able to see the centre line. This must be lined up with the toe and heel seam, so, starting at the toe, match the crease to the seam and use one pin to secure it, positioning the pin with the point towards the centre of the footpad (Fig.6) as this will make tacking the pad into position much easier. Next, line up the crease at the heel and use another pin to secure this end. Now you can pin the footpad at a point midway between the two pins on each side, making certain that the edges are absolutely level (Fig.7). This will give the effect of the pins being in the 12, 3, 6 and 9 o'clock positions of an elongated clock face. Complete the pinning of the footpad by adding pins at the 2, 4, 8 and 10 o'clock positions (Fig.8). (If you are working on a very large teddy bear such as Harvey, you may need to add further pins as required.)

When the pinning is complete, tack the footpad carefully into place and remove all the pins ready for sewing. At this stage it is important to check carefully that all the fabric edges are perfectly aligned and to make any minor adjustments that are necessary before proceeding further; once the footpad is stitched into place any irregularities or uneven edges cannot be rectified without completely replacing it, as the felt will bear

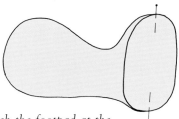

Fig.6 *Attach the footpad at the centre line, using two pins.*

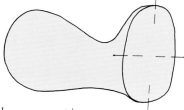

Fig.7 *Add two more pins at the sides.*

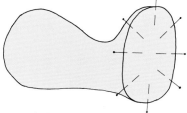

Fig.8 *Fill in with four more pins to secure the pad evenly.*

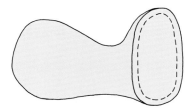

Fig.9 *Stitch around the footpad, keeping the seam allowance even.*

evidence of unpicking. However, the whole operation is not at all difficult and only needs a little care and patience for your first footpad, after which it will become very much easier.

Now the footpad is ready to be sewn into place. Starting at a point without a seam, where the material will be much less bulky, slowly stitch around the circumference of the footpad, making sure that you keep the seam allowance constant and even (Fig.9). Take your time over this and sew relatively slowly as you need to preserve the even shape and contour of the footpad – your stitching at this stage will directly affect the shape of the finished

foot. It may be easier for beginners to sew by hand, using extra-strong thread and a strong back stitch. If you are using a machine you need only use conventional sewing thread as machined seams tend to be stronger than hand-sewn ones.

Now check all the seams and if there are no gaps in the stitching and the material is completely caught into the seams, turn the leg right side out through the opening that was left during stitching of the main leg. You can now follow the same procedure to make the other leg, remembering to take plenty of time and to pin and stitch as accurately as you can as this will pay dividends on the finished result.

MAKING THE BODY

The majority of patterns in this book feature a body made from four pieces. This will give the bear a pleasing natural shape and allow for the traditional hump that is so reminiscent of the early bears. (Exceptions to the four-piece design are found in some of the miniature bears – see pages 57, 61 and 64).

Take the four body pieces that you have already cut out, making sure that you have two body fronts and two body backs with the fur pile running from top to bottom. Place a body front on top of the corresponding body back, fur sides together. The two side seams will be perfectly aligned and can be carefully pinned together from top to bottom (Fig.10). It is important that you tuck the pile in as neatly as possible with a pin as this will give a much neater finished seam. Tack along the pinned edge, remove all the pins and stitch the seam securely (Fig.11). Pull out the tacking thread and then repeat the same procedure with the remaining body back and front.

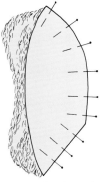 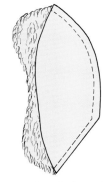

Fig.10 *Pin the front body piece to the back body piece along the side seam.*

Fig.11 *Stitch the side seams together.*

You now have two body halves that are ready to be joined together to make the complete body. To do this, place the two completed body halves fur sides together and you will see that the unsewn curved back areas are now matching. Pin these together, starting by matching the already completed side seams at the top and bottom of the body, and insert a couple of pins at these points. Continue pinning around the entire body, keeping the edges on the body front and back perfectly level and using enough pins to secure the fabric without too many puckers (Fig.12). It is best not to worry about leaving an unpinned opening in the back seam at this stage until you have gained a little experience – you will find it easier to tack the pieces into position if the seam is securely pinned all around. Using several short lengths of tacking cotton rather than one very long length which will tend to tangle easily, tack the body pieces together ready for sewing and remove the pins.

Complete the body by stitching securely around the tacked seam, starting at the top of the back opening and continuing over and around the body until you reach the bottom of the open area (Fig.13). It is important that you finish both points off securely as this opening is used for turning, jointing and stuffing. Trim off any loose thread ends and remove the tacking thread after checking that all the fabric has been caught in the seams. Turn the whole body right way out and place it to one side along with the arms and legs, awaiting the final jointing, stuffing and assembly.

MAKING THE HEAD

As with the body, the head is made in two separate stages and always comprises three main pieces – two head sides and a head gusset. The two head side pieces must first be partly joined together by placing them on a flat surface on top of each other, fur sides together, so that the straight bottom edge is facing you. With the nose of the bear pointing to your left, insert a pin at the extreme point of the nose, then start pinning from that point down until you arrive at the left-hand edge of the bottom straight edge (the neck opening), checking that the edges are level and that any pile is tucked in as you proceed (Fig.14). Tack these edges together, remove the pins and then stitch securely together (Fig.15). Pull out the tacking thread and trim off any loose stitching thread ends.

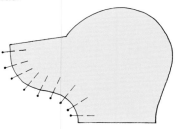

Fig.14 Pin the head side pieces together from nose to straight edge of neck.

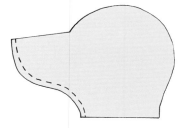

Fig.15 Stitch the head side pieces together.

The head gusset is added next to give the head its three-dimensional shape. Pin one edge of the partly joined head sides to the head gusset, fur sides together, starting at the nose and continuing along one side only, terminating at the neck edge at the back of the head (Fig.16). Pin the other edge of the head gusset in the same way to the remaining head side. Again use plenty of pins to ease the head gusset into position and when it is secured with all edges lined up, tack into place. Remove all pins and sew the head gusset into place, starting on one side at the nose and following the grain of the fur to the back of the head (Fig.17).

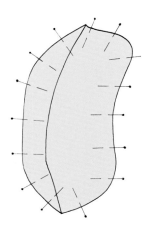

Fig.12 Pin the two body halves together.

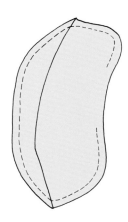

Fig.13 Stitch the body halves together leaving an opening in the back seam.

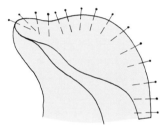

Fig.16 Pin the head gusset to one head side.

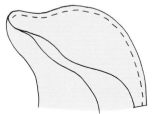

Fig.17 Sew the head gusset in place.

Repeat for the other side, again starting at the nose and leaving the bottom straight edge completely open. Examine the seams very carefully to ensure that all the fabric has been caught and there are no gaps. If there are any you must unpick the seam and resew it securely, as any unevenness will be very noticeable and will not only spoil the finished head but will make the embroidering of the nose that much more difficult. When all is satisfactory, remove the tacking thread, trim away any loose stitching thread ends and turn the head right side out through the bottom opening in the neck.

A completed head gusset.

MAKING THE EARS

The ears are the simplest part to make. Take two ear pieces and place them fur sides together, then pin together around the curved edge only, keeping the edges level and tucking in as much fur as possible with your pin (Fig.18).

Fig.18 Pin the two ear pieces together around the curved edge only.

Fig.19 Stitch around the curved edge of the ear.

Tack around this curved edge, remove the pins and stitch securely around the curved part of the ear only, leaving the bottom straight edge open (Fig. 19). Pull out the tacking thread, trim off any loose stitching thread ends and turn the ear right side out through the bottom opening. The bottom raw edges now have to be neatened and this is done by turning the raw edges under and, using extra-strong thread, oversewing the edges together (Fig.20). This should be done fairly neatly with small stitches that will not be visible on the finished bear.

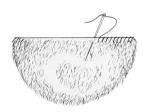

Fig.20 Oversew the raw edges of the ear together.

JOINTING AND STUFFING THE LIMBS AND HEAD

The next step is to insert the joints and stuff the bear's limbs and head. Starting with the head, the first consideration is whether you intend to fit plastic safety eyes or the traditional glass or boot-button eyes. If plastic eyes are to be fitted (essential for a child's bear) they must be secured before the head is stuffed and jointed (see Bertie bear on page 38).

Take the completed empty head and place small amounts of polyester stuffing into the nose area as firmly as possible, then continue to add stuffing little by little until the head is filled – a large handful will not only be difficult to insert through the neck opening but will result in a very uneven and soft bear as you will almost certainly end up with a lot of empty spaces that will be very difficult to reach after the head is stuffed.

As the head fills, take your stuffing stick and firm the stuffing down evenly and frequently as you work. In the early stages the stuffing will be quite springy, but as the head fills it will firm down nicely and the bear will start to take shape. It is important to make sure that the nose area is as firmly stuffed as possible, otherwise you will end up with a soft, scrunchy nose that will be difficult to embroider. At the final stages of stuffing, push the stuffing stick repeatedly from the neck cavity via the underchin area right through to the nose tip and add further stuffing in small pieces until you are happy with the firmness of the nose. This operation will appear to consume a lot of filler but you must get the head as firmly stuffed as you can, leaving the last ½ inch (12mm) of the neck area empty for jointing and closing. When the head is stuffed, check that the outside is even with no obvious lumps or hollows by firmly squeezing and shaping the head with your hands. If there are any problems, it may be necessary to remove some of the stuffing and start again to rectify the faults at this stage.

When you are completely happy that the bear's head is firm and even, the head joint is inserted. To do this, assuming you are using the traditional wooden joint (see Bertie bear on page 38 for how to use plastic safety joints) you will first have to part-

Finishing the head joint.

assemble the joint. Take one split pin, thread on one metal washer followed by the correct size wooden disc as specified by the design, then insert this half-assembled joint into the neck cavity by inverting the head and laying the joint on the stuffing (Fig.21). You will have to push down a little because of the springiness of the filler, but it is important that none of the filler is allowed to creep over the joint edge as this surface must be clear in order to allow the other joint half to sit correctly, ensuring a firm joint that will not rock from side to side.

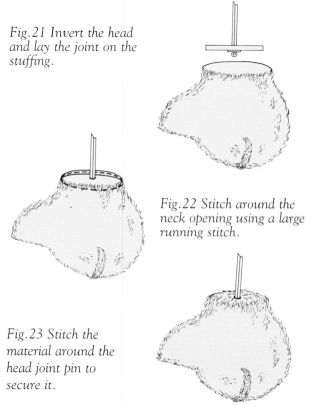

Fig.21 Invert the head and lay the joint on the stuffing.

Fig.22 Stitch around the neck opening using a large running stitch.

Fig.23 Stitch the material around the head joint pin to secure it.

With the head still inverted and the joint in position, thread a needle with a generous length of extra-strong thread, knot the end and, starting at the seam, stitch around the neck opening with a fairly large running stitch (Fig.22). Do not cut the thread at this point, as there must be sufficient thread left to allow you to pull the stitches tightly to gather the fabric around the exposed joint pin. Prevent the gathered fabric from gaping by holding it firmly in place with your thumb and stitch from side to side around the joint pin until all the fabric is secured (Fig.23). There is no need to try to achieve a perfect seamless finish with your stitching as the end result will be hidden in the final assembly stage – it is much more important that the fabric is firmly sewn in place. The exposed joint pin will not fall into the head as the firmness of the stuffing will hold it, but if you are worried about this simply splay the legs of the split pin slightly after all the stitching has been completed.

Arms and legs are very similar in the way they are jointed, the only real difference being that the arms are obviously left and right but the legs at this stage appear identical (or should do!) and are 'handed' by the position of the joints only (Fig.24).

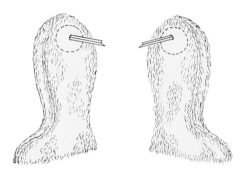

Fig.24 The legs are 'handed' by the joint positions.

To insert a joint into an arm, look inside the arm to locate the joint position that was marked before cutting out. Using your awl, make a small hole in the fabric, then assemble a half joint in the same manner as you did for the head by taking a split pin and placing a metal washer on it, followed by a wooden disc of the correct size. Insert this half joint into the arm through the opening at the back,

Stuffing an arm.

at the same time pushing the split pin out through the hole made by the awl. Push small amounts of polyester stuffing into the arm to fill the shoulder, thereby preventing the joint from further movement – use only small amounts of filler at a time as the arm is relatively narrow and must be stuffed firmly yet evenly (Fig.25). Stuffing sticks are essential for this operation – you should never use sharp-pointed metallic objects such as scissors or screwdrivers. The golden rule with all teddy bear stuffing is always to fill the hardest-to-reach areas first.

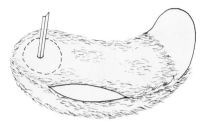

Fig.25 The arm joint in position.

The next step is to stuff the pad area, again using only small amounts of filler at a time and stuffing firmly and evenly, using your stuffing stick frequently. You need to ensure that the pads are well stuffed and very firm, just like the nose, especially if you intend to embroider some claws on your bear. However, your stuffing stick must be rounded, not sharp, as it is very easy to damage the felt or leather paw pads, in which case the only course of action would be to remake the arm and replace the pad.

You should now have an arm that has a nice firm shoulder and pad area. To finish off the middle section, add some more stuffing, this time in slightly larger amounts. Try to lay the stuffing in a lengthways direction as this will help to give rigidity to the finished arm. When the seam can be closed with a little squeeze of the fingers, the arm is filled to the right amount.

To finish the arm, the seam must be invisibly closed with a ladder stitch (Fig.26 overleaf). Thread a needle with strong thread, knot the end and, starting at the top of the opening, insert the needle from the inside edge and pull the thread through, leaving the knot firmly and invisibly anchored inside. From this point take the thread horizontally across the opening and make a small stitch on the opposite side. Repeat in the other direction and continue down the entire length of the opening, pulling the stitches as you proceed to close the seam

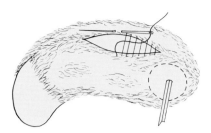

Fig.26 Close the seam with ladder stitch.

Fig.27 Pass the needle back through the final loop to make a knot.

Fig.28 Lose the thread by bringing the needle out 2 inches (5cm) away from the seam.

behind you. If you have a leather thimble, wear it on your little finger as this will allow you to pull the thread tight without your finger becoming sore. The objective is to make the stitches reasonably parallel so that the seam is neatly and firmly closed – if it is rough or puckered it will almost certainly be because your stitching is slanted, so a little extra care here is worthwhile.

When you reach the bottom, finish off by taking a final stitch and leaving it loose so that a loop remains through which the needle can be passed to create a knot (Fig.27). Do this once more and finally lose the end of the thread by inserting the needle into the arm directly next to the knot and emerging 2 inches (5cm) away (Fig.28). Pull the thread very tight, snip off at the surface and the cut end will disappear into the arm. This completes the jointing and stuffing of one arm and the second arm and the two legs are treated in exactly the same way, except that when you come to make holes for the joints in the legs you will find the marked holes are on both sides of each leg and you must remember to create a 'left' and 'right' leg.

ASSEMBLY

You have now reached the stage where your bear will start to look like a teddy bear rather than a collection of furry limbs. You should have two completed arms and legs, the head and the empty body cavity. The first step in the assembly procedure is the attachment of the head, as this provides a reference for the fitting of the limbs. The really old and valuable teddy bears tend to have the head apparently fitted in a tilted-forward position. This is often because they were originally filled with wood wool, or 'excelsior', which has collapsed slightly as a consequence of generations of love and affection and has thus caused the head to droop. In our designs in this book we have re-created this feature by fitting the head a little forward to add charm and character.

From the inside of the body, find the head joint position that was marked earlier and make a small hole with your awl. Then, taking the head, insert the legs of the split pin into the body through this hole from the outside (if you splayed the legs of the split pin earlier you will need to hold them together with a small pair of pliers while you insert the head). When the head is inserted, place the correct size wooden disc on the legs of the split pin inside the body, followed by the second metal washer, at the same time preventing the head from detaching itself from the body with your other hand.

The next step is to secure the joint and this is

Turning a wooden joint pin.

achieved by inverting the loosely fitted head and body assembly and, from the inside of the body, splaying the split pin slightly apart (Fig.29). This will prevent the joint from coming apart and give you room to turn the split pin legs with the pliers. The second metal washer that you have just fitted is perhaps the most important component as this acts as a bearing on which the turned split pin will ultimately rest, thereby preventing any wear to the wooden parts of the joint. To turn the split pin, take your long-nosed pliers, grip one of the splayed pin legs firmly and turn it tightly away from you and downwards until it is neatly rolled down in a coil on the metal washer (Fig.30).

Fig.29 Splay the split pin legs slightly apart.

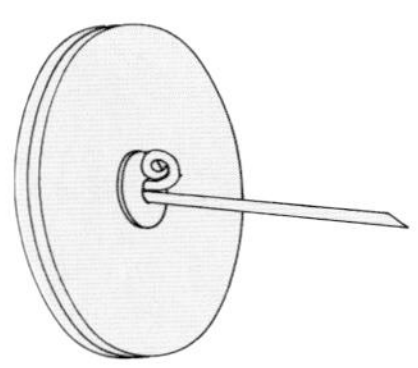

Fig.30 Roll the first pin leg down to the metal washer.

Fig.31 Roll the second pin leg down to match the first.

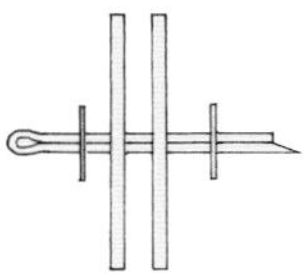

Fig.32 An exploded view of a typical wooden joint assembly.

Turn the joint so that you can treat the second split pin leg in exactly the same way so that both of them are rolled down to rest on the washer (Fig.31). Do not worry if the rolls are a little inaccurate as they will not be seen when the bear is finished, though it is important that they are not touching the wooden disc. If this is the case you will have to remake the joint as there will be rapid wear on the wooden disc, resulting in a loose joint or even joint failure. (When using traditional wooden joints [Fig.32] for the first time it is a good idea to purchase a few extra joints purely for practising on.)

When the head has been fitted, the next items to attach are the arms. From the inside of the body cavity, locate the arm joint marks and, as with the

head, make a small hole from the inside with your awl. Attach the first arm in the same way as the head, checking first that you are fitting the correct one. (If you are making one of the larger teddy bears, it is a good idea to remove a little of the mohair pile from the body and arm at the joint position, using fine scissors. This will be invisible on the finished bear as it will be under the joint but it will help to prevent the joint from wearing loose under the extra weight of the heavier limbs.) Turn the split pin legs down in exactly the same way as the head, remembering they must make contact with the metal washer.

Next fit the second arm. Before you turn the split pin legs, check that the two arms are level. If an error has crept in it can be easily rectified by removing the second arm and remaking the split pin hole accordingly – the original hole will be invisible on the finished bear as it will be covered by the joint. From time to time you may make a teddy bear from a pattern that does not have the joint positions marked on it, or you may decide that you would like to attach the limbs in a slightly different position to give your bear a personal touch. This is why the head is fitted first, as it will give a reference point to which any variations to the limbs can be made. The joint is first offered up to the body and when the limb is in a pleasing position a hole is made in the body from the outside, corresponding to the centre of the joint where the split pin protrudes. The limb is then attached in the usual way.

When assembly is completed all the limbs and the head must be checked for tightness as the material oftens puckers slightly under the joint and it must be allowed to free itself. To do this, rotate each limb in turn several times and then check that the limb can move freely with just a little effort – if it falls down under its own weight it is too loose and must be tightened. Using your long-nosed pliers, grip the offending joint split pin from inside the body and roll the legs a little tighter on to the metal washer until the desired tension is achieved. If the joint is too tight, the reverse procedure is adopted. When all adjustments have been made, rotate the limbs and head again several times for a final check before you begin to stuff the body.

STUFFING THE BODY

Now that all the limbs are attached you will see the teddy bear taking shape and the final stage is the stuffing of the body cavity. Again taking small amounts of stuffing to avoid gaps and lumps, start at the neck area and begin to fill the body, firming with the stuffing stick as you proceed. Even if you decide to have a soft-filled bear this area must be firmly stuffed to prevent the head being floppy. Continue stuffing around the shoulder and arm positions and then stop at this point and start stuffing the lower body and leg area. Again this area must be firmly stuffed to support the legs. The remaining body cavity is then filled to a suitable firmness without overfilling, but if you wish to fit a growler or 'voice' to your teddy this must be done first.

The first consideration is whether you want your teddy to growl when he is tipped backwards or forwards (or even both) – most people prefer forwards as the bear is naturally tipped forwards when cuddled.

To fit the growler forwards, place it roughly at the middle tummy area of the bear in a horizontal position with the holes in the growler facing back towards the final closing seam. Pack the stuffing firmly around the sides to prevent the growler from falling down after the bear is completed. Insert the rest of the stuffing into the cavity and cover the remaining part of the growler with sufficient filling so that it will not be felt when the seam is finally closed. If you want the growler to activate when the bear is tipped backwards the procedure is the same except that the growler holes must face forwards and the growler body is located just behind the front tummy seam, again with sufficient filling in front of the growler to prevent it being felt from outside. If your teddy bear is to be filled with wood wool or any filling that may be rather dusty the growler should be encased in a thin cotton or muslin bag before insertion to keep the mechanism free from dust which may impede operation.

When the body is filled with the correct amount of stuffing you will be able to squeeze the final seam closed relatively easily with your fingers. However, if you have overstuffed the bear the seam will not only be difficult to close but will be liable to burst open at a later date, so if necessary remove any surplus stuffing before closing the seam. The procedure is exactly the same as closing the final seams on the arms and legs.

ATTACHING THE EARS

Bears all have a character and charm of their own – some look sad and some look happy and cheeky. The determining factor is largely the size and positions of

the eyes and ears and although the patterns and illustrations give guidance there are no hard and fast rulings on the subject – all you have to remember is to keep to acceptable proportions and equal spacing.

To attach the ears, place one ear against the head in a suitable position and pin lightly into place, using three pins so that the ear is secured but can be curved forwards to give a natural appearance (Fig.33). After the first ear is roughly pinned into position, secure the second ear in the same way ensuring they look equal.

Fig.33 Use three pins to hold the ear in place prior to stitching.

Fig.34 Stitch the ear on to the head, starting at the top.

Now you can be creative and decide how you want the ears to be positioned, moving them about to give various expressions. When you are satisfied, thread a length of extra-strong thread on to a long darning needle and, starting at the top of the ear, anchor the thread to the head directly behind the ear by taking two or three very small stitches. Then take a stitch into the back of the ear followed by another stitch into the head in a similar fashion to the ladder stitch used for the seams (Fig.34). Continue down the back of the ear, using small stitches, until you arrive at the base.

To preserve the gentle curve of the ear and make stitching easier, take the next stitch by inserting the needle through the 'lobe' of the ear to the front as close to the head as possible (Fig.35). The next stitch is made through the head, passing under the ear to emerge at the back (Fig.36), followed by another stitch through the ear close to the head (Fig.37). Repeat this procedure, gradually working your way up the ear and making the final stitch at the top back. Finish off the thread in the same way as for ladder stitch. Repeat the procedure for the second ear and remove all the pins.

EMBROIDERING THE NOSE

This is the part that most novice bear-makers tend to dread and some even end up fitting a plastic nose

*Fig.35 Insert
the needle
through the lobe
of the ear.*

*Fig.36 Pass the
needle under the
ear to emerge at
the back.*

*Fig.37 Take
another stitch
through the ear,
close to the
head.*

and as close as possible to the glued template and pass the needle through the nose under the template area to emerge at a point on the opposite side of the template, again as close as possible to the template edge (A) (Fig.38 overleaf). Pull the nose thread through until the end just disappears into the head, then insert the needle directly into the same hole it has just emerged from and again pass under and across the nose template (B). Repeat two or three times (C) to secure the thread and direct the needle to emerge on the final pass at a point roughly ¼ inch (7mm) below the template on the centre seam (D).

From this point, take the first stitch directly up to the top edge of the felt template and enter the head to pass back down under the template, emerge at the same point at the bottom (E). Take a second stitch directly over the first, entering the template at the top and emerging again alongside the first two stitches at the base of the template (F). Repeat this process making sure that each successive stitch is lying parallel to the previous stitch (G), slowly working your way out to one side of the template following its outline top and bottom until you reach the outside edge of the nose.

At the outside edge, insert the needle at the top edge of the template on its final stitch and emerge to the other side of the first two central stitches (H). Follow the same procedure for the other side (I) until you again arrive at the end of the template. On the final vertical stitch, insert the needle at the corner of the template to emerge at a point where you wish the bottom inverted 'V' of the mouth to start (J). Then pass the needle under the two first stitches which are roughly ¼ inch (7mm) from the bottom of the template (K) and reinsert it at a point directly opposite where it emerged from on the other side to form the completed 'V' of your bear's mouth (L).

To finish off, pass the needle backwards and forwards through the head (M) invisibly two or three times in the same manner as the anchoring at the start (N,O), pull the thread quite tightly and snip it close to the pile backing to allow the loose end to retract into the head. If you do have any difficulties in pulling your needle through, the long-nosed pliers used for jointing will be useful for gripping the needle, particularly in those bears that may have a slightly bulky seam from the sewing stage.

to avoid the embroidering altogether. However, our method is very simple and virtually foolproof. The first step is to take your felt nose template and lightly pin it into position on the nose. Experiment with minor changes of position to suit your taste, but make sure the nose is central.

The next step is to remove the felt template and trim away the surplus mohair that will be directly beneath it, using a small pair of pointed scissors. Trim this section right down to the backing fabric and when it is completely free from fur, glue the felt nose template into position with a fabric glue. Allow the glue to dry completely before proceeding to the next stage.

Now take a large-diameter darning needle and thread it with a double thickness of your chosen nose thread, making it approximately 30–40 inches (76–102cm) in length when doubled. Do not knot it. Before you can start embroidering, you must first invisibly secure the end of the nose thread. To do this, insert the needle into the nose at the very edge

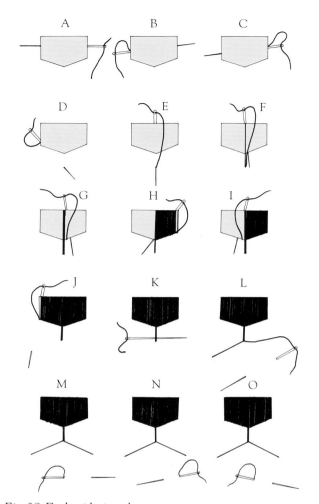

Fig.38 *Embroidering the nose.*

FITTING GLASS EYES

For collectors' teddy bears the most favoured eyes are glass, although these should not be used if the bear is intended for a child. The majority of glass eyes are handmade and there can be variances in dimensions and shapes, even between a pair of eyes purchased on a wire, so if you are making bears in large numbers it is best to purchase eyes in quantities of ten pairs or so in order to match them into pairs before fitting.

Assuming your eyes are the one-piece wire type, which is the most common, your first task is to prepare them prior to fitting. Using a pair of wire cutters or similar, separate the eyes by cutting the centre of the wire (Fig.39) then, taking each eye in turn, form a secure loop for attaching the eye into the head of your bear. To do this, gently bend the remaining short length in half without creasing it to form the start of the loop (Fig.40). Holding the end

of the wire against the fixed part at the eye end, insert a match or cocktail stick into the loop and wind up the wire to form a twist, not too tightly – you only need three or four twists. The match or cocktail stick will act as a former and the result will be a neat twist with an evenly formed loop (Fig. 41). This is secure enough, but you can lightly solder the twist in place for added peace of mind.

Your next task is to choose the position of the eyes. An easy way to do this is to take a spare pair of eyes of a similar size and colour that have about a ½ inch (12mm) wire on the back but with no loop formed. Lightly press the eyes into position by inserting the wire into the head, and keep on repositioning them until you are happy with the expression. Withdraw the trial eye slightly and insert the awl at the point of entry made by the short wire, then remove the eye completely and make a hole of sufficient diameter to accept the loop on the eye that is to be fitted.

To prepare the eye for fixing, cut a piece of the extra-strong thread long enough that when doubled it will pass diagonally through the head of your bear with plenty of spare thread to allow you to finish off. Loop the thread through the loop of the glass eye (Fig. 42), then attach it by passing the thread ends through the thread loop (Fig. 43) and pulling tight.

Fig.39 *The wire of the glass eye cut ready for looping.*

Fig.40 *Bend the wire in half to form the start of the loop.*

Fig.41 *The finished loop neatly twisted.*

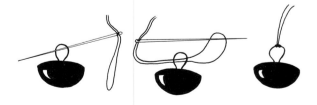

Fig.42 *Pass the thread through the wire loop.*

Fig.43 *Pass the thread ends through the thread loop.*

Fig.44 *Knot the thread on top of the wire loop.*

If you wish you can knot the thread on top of the loop to secure it further (Fig. 44). Then thread the two thread ends on to an extra-long needle and insert it into the hole made by the awl. Pass the needle through the head so that it emerges at a point midway behind the opposite ear (Fig. 45).

To finish off, replace the long needle with a shorter, fine darning needle and place a thumb on the eye to exert a little pressure while you pull the thread very tightly. This will cause the eye to create a small depression in the head and form its own natural-looking socket. Take a small stitch behind the ear and pull the thread through to form a loop, then pass the needle through it to create a neat knot as the loop is pulled tight (Fig. 46). Repeat this two or three times and then snip the thread close to the pile backing.

Do exactly the same for the other eye, but before securing it double-check that it is level with the first eye. An alternative method is to finish off at the base of the neck instead of behind the ear. Whichever method you use, it is important that each eye is secured at a point diagonally opposite, as this will ensure a natural appearance to the eye. Eyes that are finished off on the same side of the head may give the bear a squint.

Fig.45 Pass the needle through the head to emerge at the opposite ear.

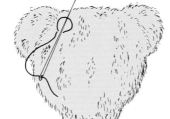

Fig.46 Pass the needle through the looped thread to finish off.

GROOMING

The last step is the grooming of your bear. No matter how careful you have been, some seams will be showing where the pile has been caught in the seams at the sewing stage. This is easily rectified with a teasel brush. Holding the brush lightly but firmly, brush along the seams against the direction of the pile and the seams will disappear like magic as the bristles lift the trapped pile. Take particular care around the paw pads, nose embroidery and eyes as the wire bristles will damage these very easily. An alternative to the teasel brush is a pet grooming brush but if neither of these is available you could use the point of a pin or fine needle to achieve the same effect, albeit a little slower.

The muzzle area will probably need to be tidied by snipping away the unwanted pile around the nose and, usually, the sides of the muzzle. To do this, take a small pair of sharp pointed scissors and gently snip away the pile, ensuring that the cuts are always in the direction of the pile. Take your time and make only small cuts, graduating them from the short fur at the nose and allowing the clipping to blend into the longer pile further back on the face. This trimming sounds drastic, but it will give your bear a professional look. If you prefer you can practise on a scrap of fur beforehand until you feel confident enough to tackle the real thing. Don't ever be tempted to use electric shavers or dog grooming clippers, as even when you are experienced they are too fast and severe.

Now all that needs to be done to your teddy bear is to add a little something that will make him special – perhaps a silk or satin ribbon, a bow tie, or even a little collar with a bell. The variety of finishes to personalize teddy bears is endless and this is your chance to make your bear truly an individual.

Clipping the muzzle areas.

BRING ON
THE BEARS

BERTIE BEAR

Bertie is a good introduction to making traditional jointed teddy bears as his short limbs and muzzle and curved arms make him very economical for practising upon. This style of teddy bear design was in fact developed as a cost-cutting measure by some teddy bear manufacturers in the postwar years. This 15 inch (380mm) fully jointed bear is made from synthetic fur fabric, although you can use mohair fabric if you wish. However, as synthetic furs are considerably less expensive, it is a good idea to use one if this your first attempt at teddy bear-making – and, along with the safety eyes and joints, this will make Bertie a suitable bear to give to a child.

MATERIALS

½yd (45cm) ⅜ inch (8mm) pile fur fabric

5 x 1¾ inch (45mm) plastic safety joints

1 pair ⅝ inch (15mm) plastic safety eyes

5½yd (5m) black nose thread

1lb (500g) polyester stuffing

6 x 12 inches (150 x 300mm) wool mix felt for pads

small piece black felt for nose template

1 reel sewing thread (to match fur fabric)

1 reel extra-strong thread (to match fur fabric)

1 Follow the instructions on pages 20–21 for making your pattern templates and cutting out the materials.

2 As the arms are probably the easiest part to make, it is best to deal with these first if you are a novice. Follow the instructions on page 21 to assemble the

paw pad to the inner arm. This can then be pinned to the outer arm piece and tacked and stitched in place. When the stitched arm is turned, the next step is to insert the correct size of safety joint. From the inside of the arm, locate the marked joint position and with an awl, make a hole through the fabric large enough to accept the plastic shank of the joint. Then from the inside, insert the half of the joint that has the shank moulded to it into the arm to allow the shank to emerge through the hole in the fabric and position the joint to lie flat. Then stuff the arm, following the instructions on page 27 and making sure that the joint is initially held flat to the fabric until sufficient filler is introduced to hold it firmly in place. Assemble the second arm.

3 Next assemble the legs and the footpads (see pages 22 and 23). When the completed legs are stitched and turned, insert the plastic safety joints in exactly the same manner as the arms but do remember that the legs only become left and right legs by the positioning of the joints. Stuff the legs and close the final seam.

4 The head is straightforward – follow the instructions on pages 24–25. The next step is the fitting of the plastic safety eyes. The easiest way to align the eyes accurately is to stuff the head firmly to obtain the final shape. Then, using an awl, make a hole for one eye only and insert the shank of the eye so that the eye is fitted flush to the head, but not yet secured. If you are happy with the position of this eye, place the second eye level and equally spaced to the first and when you have found the correct position, make a second hole with the awl and place this eye also flush to the head. Gently remove all of the head stuffing without disturbing the eyes and then simply attach the security washers to the shanks of the eyes to fix them permanently into position (see Fig.1). Restuff the head.

5 Stitch the body together (see pages 23-24) and turn it ready for the final assembly of the bear.

6 Assemble the bear in the way described on pages 28–29, remembering that the head is the key reference point and must be attached first. As you will be using plastic safety joints, the tightening procedures in the wooden jointing instructions will

Fig.1 The position of the security washer of a safety eye.

not apply. Instead, the plastic joints are held with one-way security washers that once fitted will not come off, so if you make a mistake during assembly you will have to saw the joint off and fit a replacement. When all the five items are assembled, rotate every limb and head for several minutes before stuffing the body cavity. This will then show up any joints that are a little loose, in which case you will need to apply a little extra pressure to the securing washer on the shanks of the joints. The easiest way to do this is with the aid of a joint safety tool designed for this purpose, but if you cannot buy one an empty cotton reel spool will do.

7 Stuff the bear (see pages 29–30) and close the final seam, then add the ears and nose (see pages 30–31). If you are using synthetic fur fabric, you will not need to trim the muzzle except the part immediately under the nose template itself.

8 Finally, give the completed bear a grooming with a soft brush to lift out any of the fur pile that may have become trapped in the seams. The addition of a short length of ribbon would be a nice finishing touch to your first teddy bear.

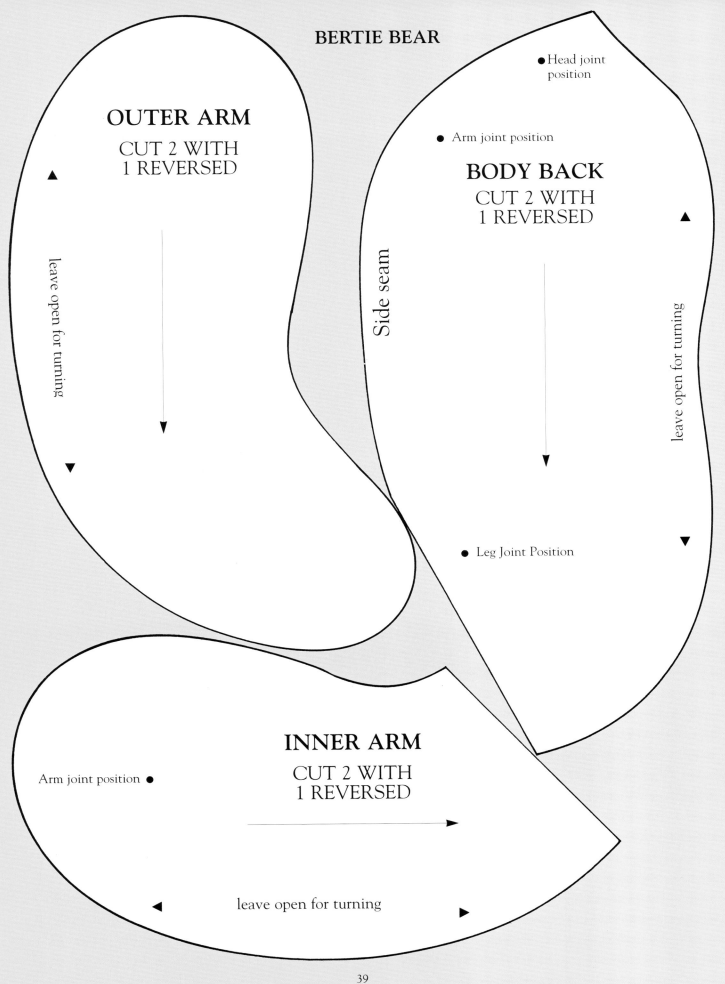

BERTIE BEAR

OUTER ARM

CUT 2 WITH
1 REVERSED

leave open for turning

Head joint position

Arm joint position

BODY BACK

CUT 2 WITH
1 REVERSED

Side seam

leave open for turning

Leg Joint Position

INNER ARM

CUT 2 WITH
1 REVERSED

Arm joint position

leave open for turning

BERTIE BEAR

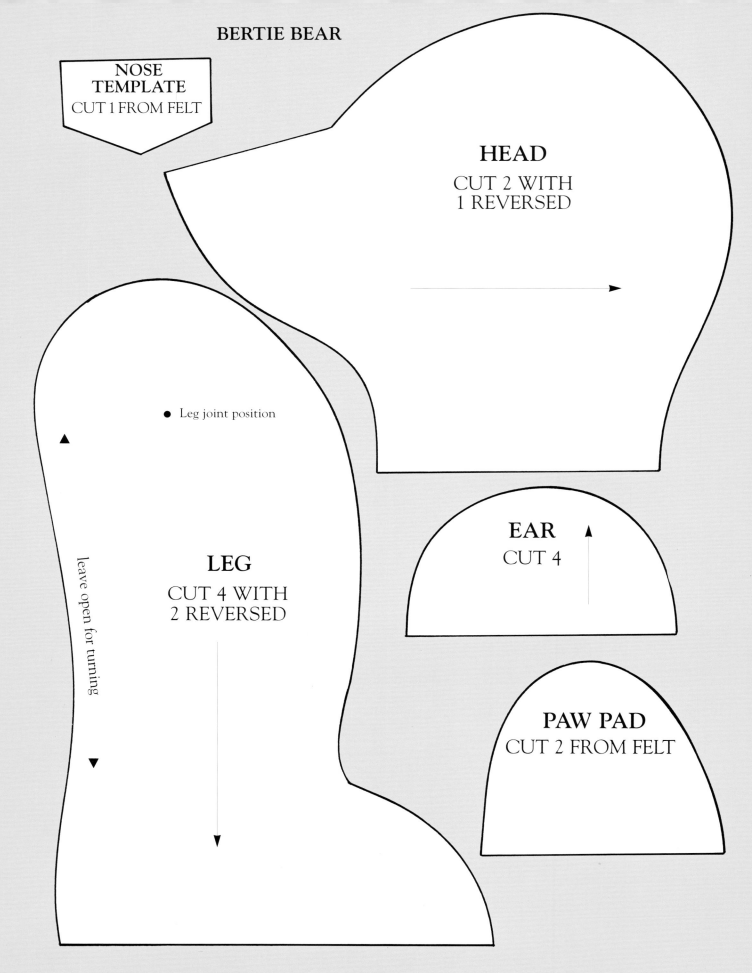

NOSE TEMPLATE
CUT 1 FROM FELT

HEAD
CUT 2 WITH
1 REVERSED

● Leg joint position

LEG
CUT 4 WITH
2 REVERSED

leave open for turning

EAR
CUT 4

PAW PAD
CUT 2 FROM FELT

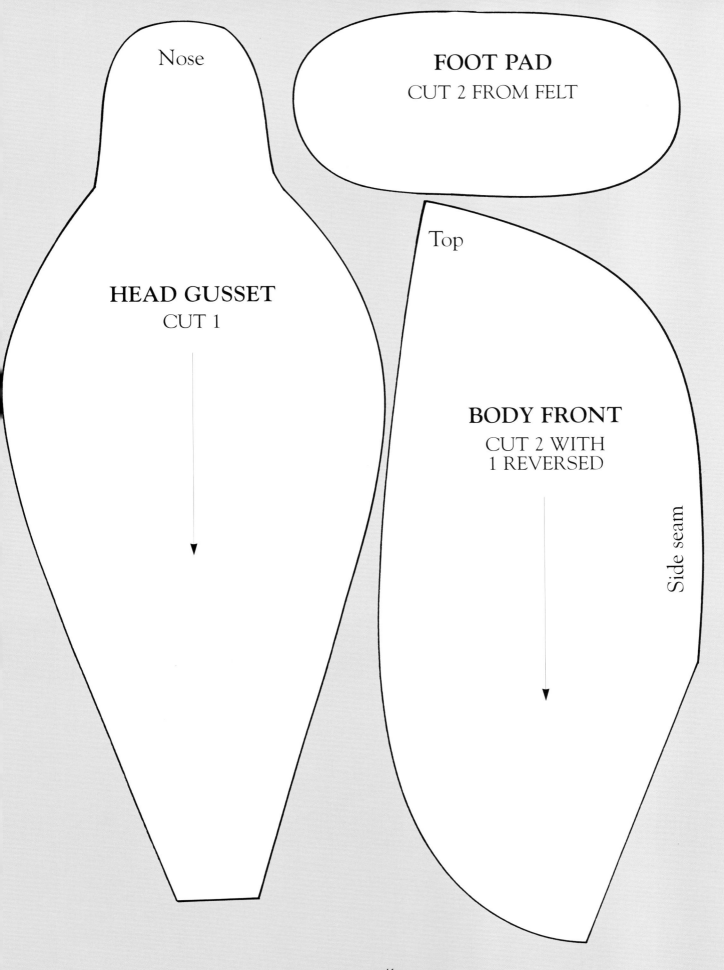

Nose

FOOT PAD
CUT 2 FROM FELT

Top

HEAD GUSSET
CUT 1

BODY FRONT

CUT 2 WITH
1 REVERSED

Side seam

HAYDN MUSICAL BEAR

This 14 inch (356mm) mohair teddy is a bear with a difference – he plays a tune! This is simply a clockwork musical movement operated by a key in the traditional music box fashion. Haydn has a slightly humped back to facilitate the fitting of the movement and the long arms so very popular on early teddy bears. This bear also has a horizontally embroidered nose and some very unusual web-design claws on his paws similar to those used on some of the early British teddy bears from around 1920.

MATERIALS

¼yd (25cm) ½ inch (12mm) pile German embossed mohair

5 x 1½ inch (36mm) wooden joints

1 pair ½ inch (12mm) black glass eyes

5 ½yd (5m) black nose thread

1lb (500g) polyester stuffing

1 x 12-note plastic 'shelled' key-operated musical movement

6 x 12 inches (150 x 300mm) wool mix felt for pads

1 reel sewing thread (to match fur fabric)

1 reel extra-strong thread (to match fur fabric)

1 Follow instructions on pages 20–21 for making pattern templates and cutting out the materials.

2 Assemble the legs and the arms (see page 21–23), remembering when inserting the leg joints to make a left- and right-handed pair.

3 The head is assembled as in the instructions on pages 24–25. As the nose on this design is stitched horizontally rather than vertically, it is important when you are pinning the head gusset to the two head sides that you ensure the three pieces are a good even fit as your finished seams will provide a guide when stitching the nose. Try to stitch them in place with no puckers or excessive seam allowances that could cause you problems when embroidering the nose later. If you want to use plastic safety eyes instead of glass, remember to fix them in position before the head is stuffed.

4 This bear has a four-piece body and as he is designed to accept the musical movement correct identification of the pieces is important. Make sure they are correctly positioned and aligned before the pinning and sewing. Turn the completed body through the opening in the back seam and trim off any loose threads.

5 The bear is completely jointed as instructed on pages 28–29. Check the tightness and security of all the joints by rotating them several times and if necessary tighten securely before any stuffing of the body is attempted.

6 Stuff the bear (see pages 29–30), remembering the golden rule of first stuffing those areas that are furthest away from the seam and consequently the hardest to reach. Use the stuffing stick to firm down the stuffing frequently, especially at the head and shoulder areas and also at the bottom of the bear where the legs are attached. Failure to stuff either of these two areas firmly enough will result in the finished bear not being able to support its head or

legs. Leave some space at the back of the bear to accommodate the musical movement unit. When you buy the movement make sure it is of the plastic-cased or 'shelled' type as some are sold for fitting into musical jewellery boxes with the mechanism exposed and these are not suitable for soft toys. Position the unit so that the key will emerge through the final seam and then pack a small amount of stuffing around and on top of the unit so that it cannot be felt through the fabric from the back. Close the final seam with a ladder stitch, working around the key and finishing off tightly.

Closing the final seam around the musical movement.

7 After the eyes and ears have been fitted, the nose can be embroidered in the following manner. No template is needed for this nose as the seams of the head gusset provide the guide for stitching. To start, thread a needle with sufficient nose thread and attach the end securely (see page 31). When you have determined how large the nose is to be, bring your needle out at the point on the head gusset seam where the top of your nose is to start. Insert your needle again into the head gusset seam directly opposite the first point, then pass the needle back through the nose just under the surface to emerge as close as possible below the first point (Fig.1). This will give a flat horizontal stitch which will be the top first line of the embroidery. Repeat the process (Fig.2), working slowly and evenly down the nose

Fig.1 Taking the first stitch in a horizontal nose. *Fig.2 Continue with parallel horizontal stitches.*

to terminate at the natural bottom nose point of the head gusset. You should now have a perfectly formed triangular nose ready for the addition of the final stages of the mouth (see page 31).

8 Finally, the paws should be embroidered to complete this bear. Follow the instructions given for Marmaduke bear (see page 112) to embroider four claws but allow a little extra amount of thread. Bring the needle out at the point shown in Fig. 3A and follow the sequence carefully. After the four webs are complete, finish off in the usual way and repeat for the other paw. Then give Haydn a final grooming with a teasel brush to lift any pile trapped in the seams, paying particular care around the eyes, paws and pads and of course any embroidered parts.

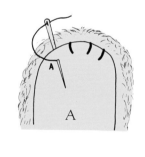
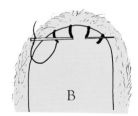
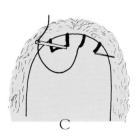
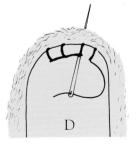

Fig.3 Embroidering web paw pads.

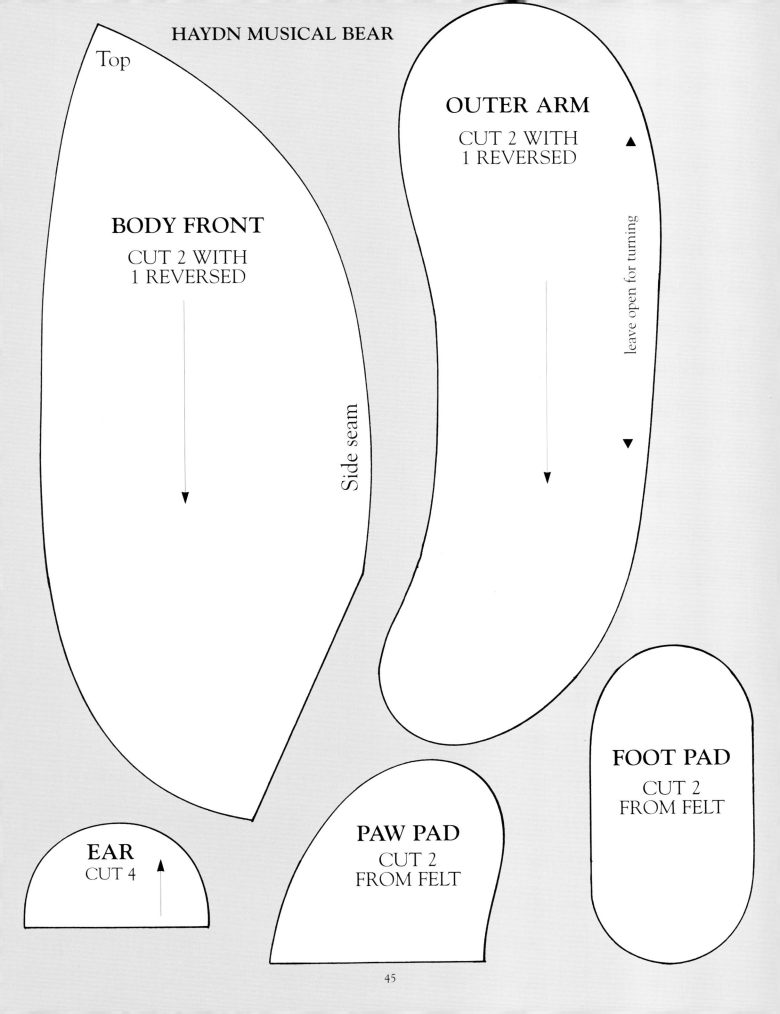

HAYDN MUSICAL BEAR

Top

BODY FRONT

CUT 2 WITH
1 REVERSED

Side seam

OUTER ARM

CUT 2 WITH
1 REVERSED

leave open for turning

FOOT PAD

CUT 2
FROM FELT

EAR
CUT 4

PAW PAD

CUT 2
FROM FELT

45

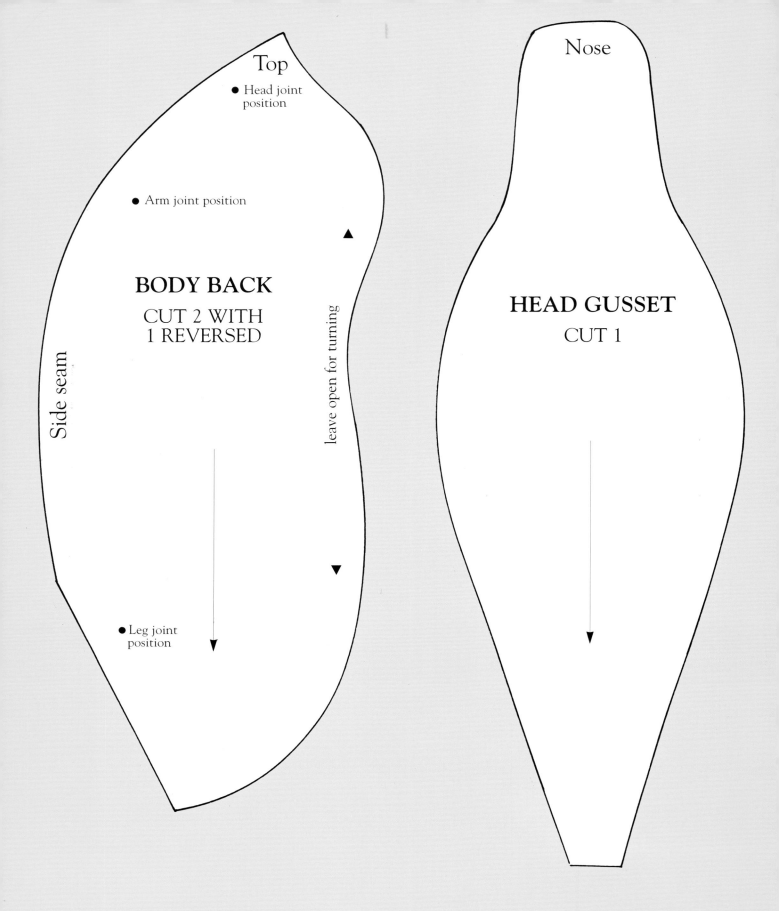

Top

● Head joint
position

● Arm joint position

▲

BODY BACK

**CUT 2 WITH
1 REVERSED**

Side seam

leave open for turning

▼

● Leg joint
position

Nose

HEAD GUSSET

CUT 1

HAYDN MUSICAL BEAR

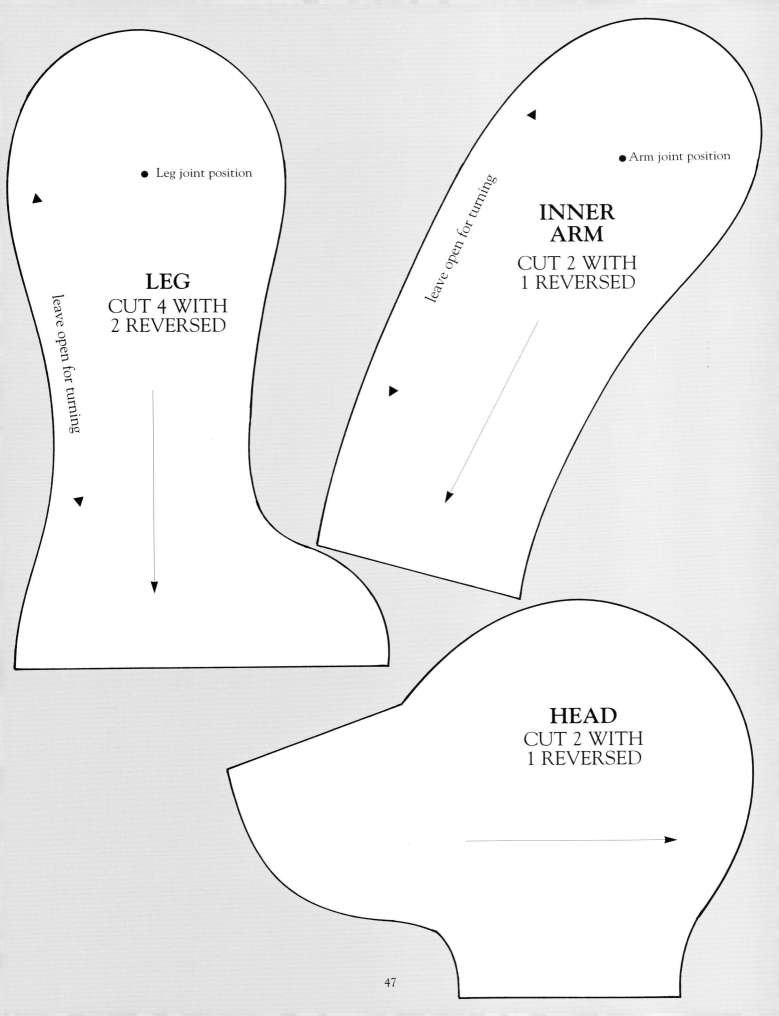

● Leg joint position

LEG
CUT 4 WITH
2 REVERSED

leave open for turning

◀ Arm joint position

INNER ARM
CUT 2 WITH
1 REVERSED

leave open for turning

HEAD
CUT 2 WITH
1 REVERSED

EDWIN BEAR

Edwin is 16 inches (400mm) tall, with a slight hump on his back and long arms but fairly short legs. The pads on the arms have a slightly different shape from the norm and a further individual touch is that the glass eyes have been painted, re-creating a technique used on some teddy bears manufactured around 1907. This procedure is useful if you cannot obtain a coloured glass eye that will co-ordinate with your chosen fabric, and it also gives you the freedom to buy a selection of eye sizes for future bears without worrying about eye colours. Finally, Edwin's ears are attached in a different way – they are sewn into slits cut into the side of the head and then stitched into a curved and very permanent position.

MATERIALS

½ yd (45cm) ½ inch (12mm) pile German embossed mohair

5 x 2 inch (50mm) wooden joints

1 pair ⅝ inch (15mm) clear glass eyes

5½yd (5m) brown nose thread

1½lb (750g) polyester stuffing

6 x 12 inches (150 x 300mm) wool mix felt for pads

small piece brown felt for nose template

small jar enamel or acrylic paint for eye backs

small artist's paintbrush

1 reel sewing thread (to match fur fabric)

1 reel extra-strong thread (to match fur fabric)

1 Follow instructions on pages 20–21 for making pattern templates and cutting out the materials.

Ears inserted in slits in the head.

2 Make up the arms, legs and body in the normal way (see pages 21–24).

3 Next sew together the four ear pieces so that you have two completed ears and turn them right side out. For this method of ear fitting you do not need to oversew the bottom raw edges together. At this stage, as on all the bears in this book, there is no left or right ear – they are interchangeable and you have the choice of which side of the ear looks best to face forwards. This is useful with distressed mohair, on which the pile sometimes appears to lie in different directions. Take one of the head side pieces with the ear slit already cut as shown on the pattern and insert an ear into the slit by laying the head piece fur side up and placing the ear on the head side, aligning the raw edge of the ear with the raw edges of the slit. Fold the head back over the ear, ensuring that the raw edges are still aligned. Pin into place and stitch securely, then open the head side flat again. You will see that the ear appears to be far too long for the slit and approximately one-third of it extends above the top edge of the head side. Bend this exposed part of the ear forward towards the point of the nose, line up the raw edges with the top of the head side and pin them into place. Tack the edges together and then repeat for the other head side and ear. Assemble the two head sides and the head gusset (see pages 24–25) and pin the three pieces into position ready for tacking. The ears will simply be secured during the normal head gusset stitching process. If you prefer, the ears can be attached in the simpler method (see page 30), remembering that the raw edges of the ears will need oversewing together first and of course, the slits in the head sides are left uncut.

4 When the bear has been assembled, stuffed and the nose embroidered (see pages 28–31), the eyes can be attached. For this bear, the eyes are of the clear glass type with a solid black pupil, available from specialist teddy bear suppliers. Take one of the eyes and, using a soft cloth, gently clean the back to remove any greasy fingermarks. Using a small artist's paintbrush, apply a little paint to the back of the eye only, starting by painting over the black pupil area and working outwards. Turn the eye over to see the effect achieved; if the colour is as you wish, continue painting the eye up to, but not over, the edge. The reflection of the glass will distribute the colour sufficiently without your risking overpainting the edge of the eye. If the colour is not as you imagined, you can remove the paint relatively easily before it dries and, after cleaning with a suitable solvent, simply re-paint with a different colour. Acrylic paint is more convenient as it is water soluble while wet and brushes can be easily cleaned in warm clean water. Leave both eyes to dry overnight and then simply fix in the normal way (see pages 32–33).

5 Finally, groom the bear with a teasel brush, lifting the trapped pile from the seams, and attach a nice satin bow to complete him.

Painting glass eyes.

EDWIN BEAR

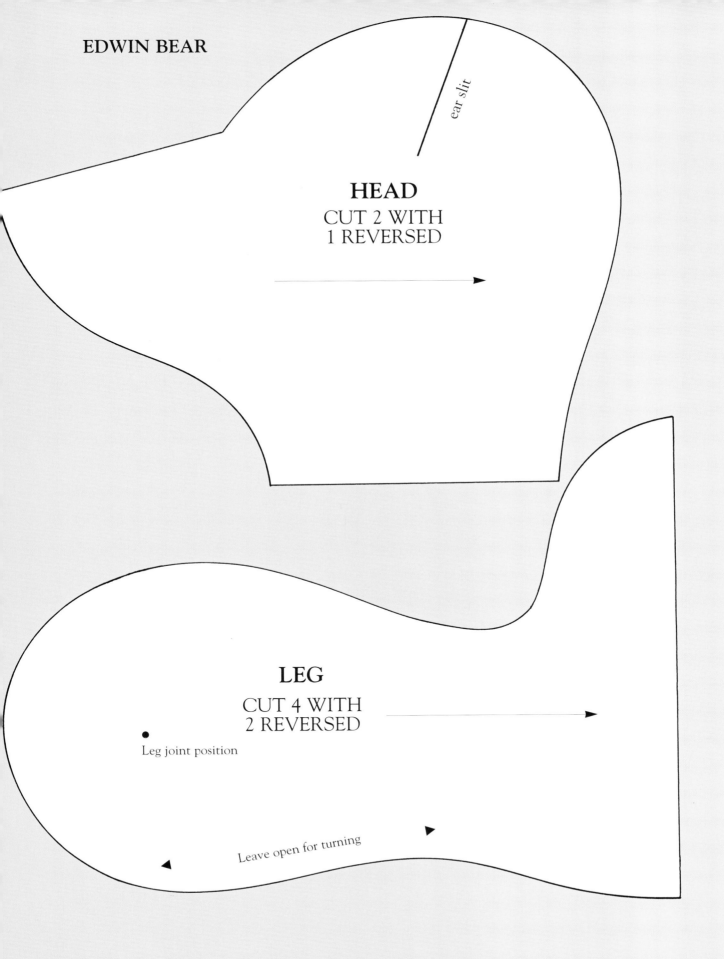

ear slit

HEAD
CUT 2 WITH
1 REVERSED

LEG
CUT 4 WITH
2 REVERSED

Leg joint position

Leave open for turning

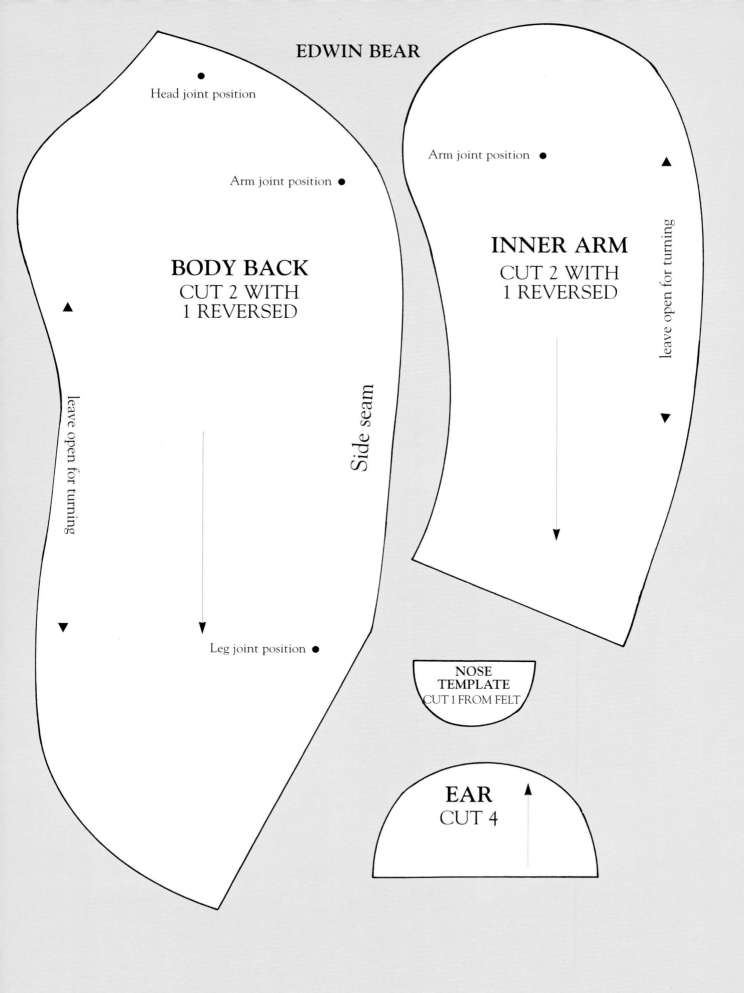

EDWIN BEAR

Head joint position

Arm joint position

BODY BACK
CUT 2 WITH
1 REVERSED

leave open for turning

Side seam

Leg joint position

INNER ARM
CUT 2 WITH
1 REVERSED

Arm joint position

leave open for turning

**NOSE
TEMPLATE**
CUT 1 FROM FELT

EAR
CUT 4

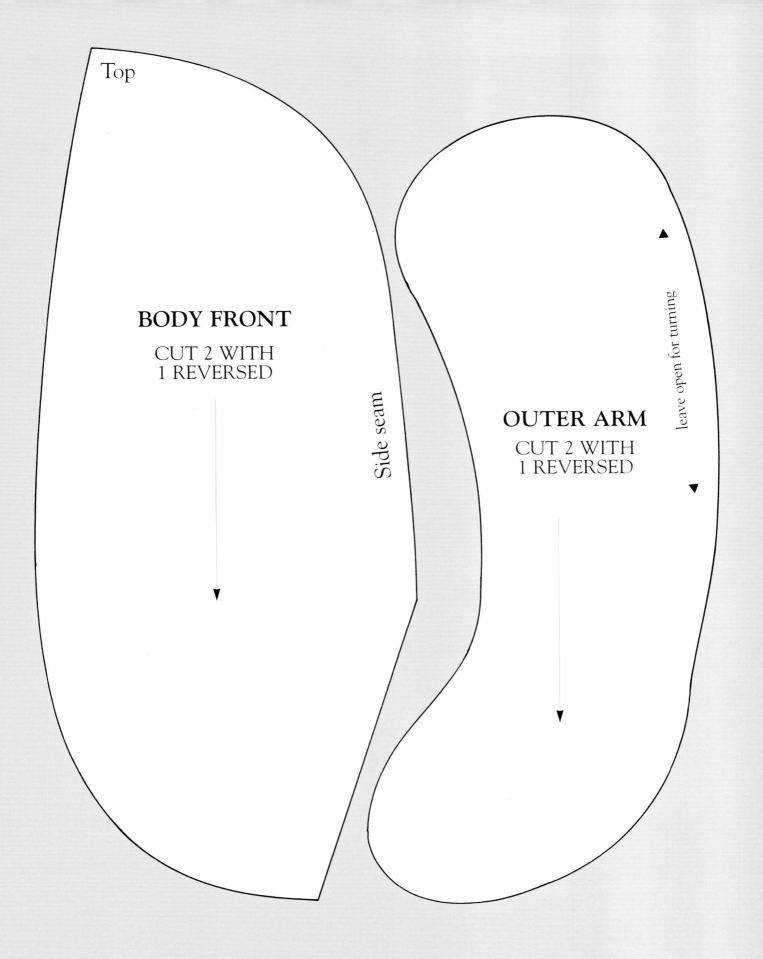

Top

BODY FRONT

CUT 2 WITH
1 REVERSED

Side seam

OUTER ARM

CUT 2 WITH
1 REVERSED

leave open for turning

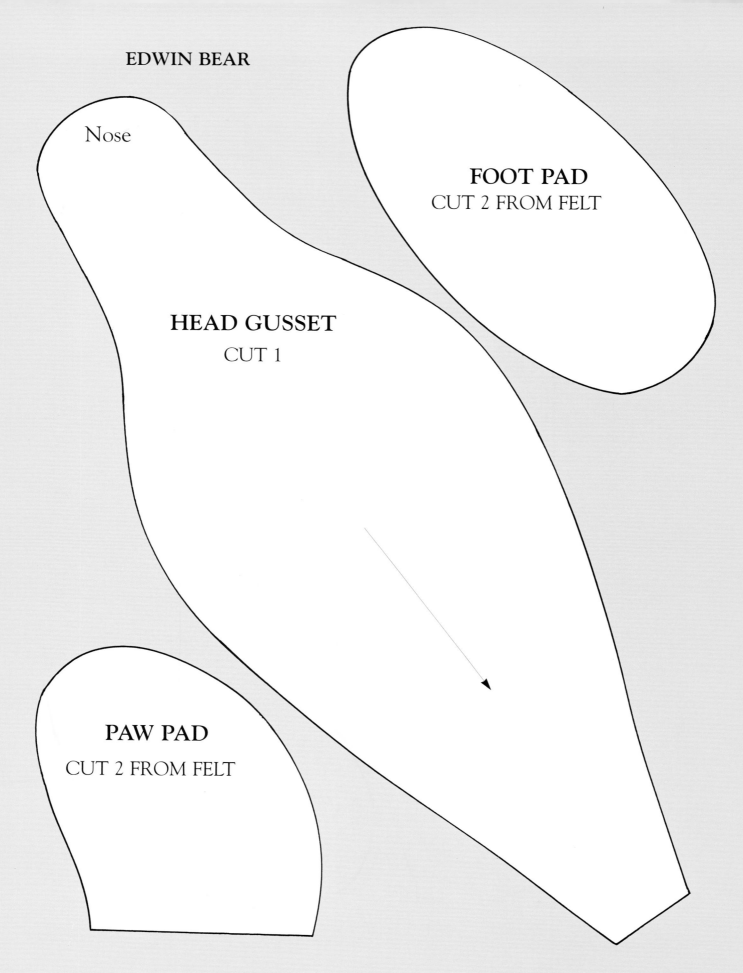

EDWIN BEAR

Nose

HEAD GUSSET

CUT 1

FOOT PAD

CUT 2 FROM FELT

PAW PAD

CUT 2 FROM FELT

BARNABY BEAR

At only 7 inches (180mm), Barnaby is the first of three miniature bears featured in the book. This delightful little chap features a two-piece body design and can be made from the leftover pieces of material from larger projects that otherwise might go to waste. He is especially suitable as a mascot bear and would make a lovely little present for somebody to treasure. Although the design uses glass eyes and traditional wooden joints, you can of course use plastic safety eyes and joints if the bear is intended for a child. Here he has not been given clothes, but if he is to be a mascot a little imagination and a few scraps of material will easily transform him into whatever character you wish.

MATERIALS

¼ yd (25cm) ⅜ inch (8mm) pile distressed mohair
5 x ¾ inch (18mm) wooden joints
1 pair ¼ inch (7mm) black glass eyes
2 yd (1.8m) black nose thread
¼ lb (125g) polyester stuffing
6 x 6 inches (150 x 150mm) felt for pads
small piece black felt for nose template
small squeaker (optional)
1 reel sewing thread (to match fur fabric)
1 reel extra-strong thread (to match fur fabric)

1 Follow the instructions on pages 20–21 for making your pattern templates and cutting out the materials.

2 The arms, legs and head are quite straightforward and should be made up in the usual way (see pages 21–25), remembering that if you wish to use plastic safety eyes these need to be fitted before the head is stuffed by following the instructions for fitting safety eyes to Bertie bear (page 38).

3 The body on this bear is different to the four-piece bear designs covered so far, as for the smaller bears a two-piece body is a little more practical and easier to sew. Before sewing the body, first prepare a body piece by folding it in half lengthways with the fur sides together and secure it in this position with one pin at the top and a second one at the bottom of the body (Fig.1). Then tack along the dart line which you should have marked on the fabric at the template stage before cutting your pieces out. (If this was overlooked, unpin the body side and, using the template, mark accordingly.) Stitch the darts along these lines (Fig.2), remove the tacking thread and trim the excess fabric in the dart to remove the bulk approximately ⅜ inch (7mm) from the

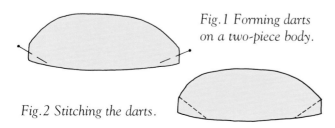

Fig.1 Forming darts on a two-piece body.

Fig.2 Stitching the darts.

stitching line. Repeat the process for the remaining body side and when this is complete pin the two pieces right sides together, lining up the dart seams at the top and bottom of the body. Using a pin or needle, push as much of the pile as possible back into the seam as you pin as this will give a more professional finish and will ease the grooming at the finishing stage. Tack these two sides into place and stitch all the way around, leaving the opening free for turning and jointing as marked on the pattern.

4 After turning the body fur side out, the bear is assembled in the usual way (see pages 28–29), starting of course with the head which is essential for your reference point. When all the necessary adjustments to the head, arm and leg joints are completed, the bear is ready to be stuffed.

5 The stuffing of the bear is quite straightforward as in the instructions on pages 29–30 and as long as the leg, head and shoulder areas are nicely even and firmly stuffed you may proceed to fill the rest of the cavity. A squeaker may be fitted at this stage, especially if the bear is for a small child. To do this, lightly stuff the body cavity at the front of the bear with just enough stuffing to prevent the squeaker from being felt from the outside. Lay the squeaker flat on top of this and proceed to stuff the rest of the bear. A variation to the normal polyester stuffing of these smaller teddy bears is the addition of a quantity of plastic or p.v.c. pellets to the partially stuffed body cavity to add weight and cause the body to sag a little, although this is not recommended if the bear is to be given to a child. For details of how to do this, see Alonzo bear on page 67.

6 Now attach the ears (see pages 30) and the glass eyes (see pages 32–33). Embroider the nose in the conventional way (see pages 31–32). If you would prefer the horizontal nose shown on Haydn, follow the instructions on page 44.

7 You need to take extra care if you are using a teasel brush for the final grooming of a bear of this small size, especially around the eyes and pad areas. If you prefer, these areas can be groomed with a needle or pin to remove the fur trapped in the seams and will be almost as quickly done as with a teasel brush because of their small size.

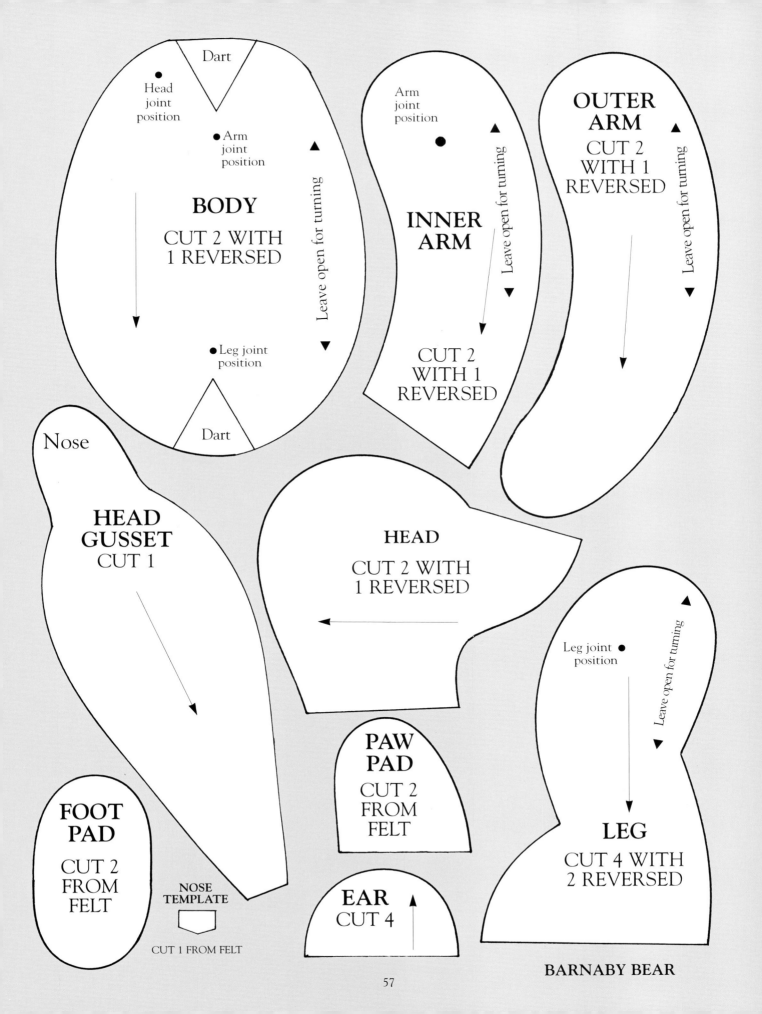

Dart

Head joint position

Arm joint position

BODY
CUT 2 WITH 1 REVERSED

Leave open for turning

Leg joint position

Dart

Arm joint position

INNER ARM

Leave open for turning

CUT 2 WITH 1 REVERSED

OUTER ARM
CUT 2 WITH 1 REVERSED

Leave open for turning

Nose

HEAD GUSSET
CUT 1

HEAD
CUT 2 WITH 1 REVERSED

Leg joint position

Leave open for turning

FOOT PAD
CUT 2 FROM FELT

NOSE TEMPLATE

CUT 1 FROM FELT

PAW PAD
CUT 2 FROM FELT

EAR
CUT 4

LEG
CUT 4 WITH 2 REVERSED

BARNABY BEAR

JASPER BEAR

This 5 inch (125mm) bear (shown top right and bottom left, opposite) is the second of the three miniature bears in this book. Like Barnaby, he is fully jointed and a very economical to make, although for best results you will need to purchase miniature teddy bear mohair and kapok for the stuffing. If you have any difficulty in obtaining the correct mohair fabric, do not despair as Jasper does look rather cute when made from good-quality velvet. Making this bear will be easier if you obtain a pair of forceps or seizers, a pair of miniature round-nosed pliers and, for stuffing, a wooden manicure stick – try to find one which has a different shape at either end. Because this bear is so small it is not practical to sew him by machine. However, you will find that sewing by hand is rather restful and as he is only small and has one-piece folded legs and arms he is very quick to make.

MATERIALS

12 x 12 inches (300 x 300mm) ³⁄₁₆ inch (4mm) pile mini bear mohair

5 x ¼ inch (7mm) fibreboard joints

1 pair ³⁄₁₆ inch (4mm) black glass eyes

2 yd (1.8m) nose thread

¼lb (125g) kapok stuffing

6 x 6 inches (150 x 150mm) felt for pads

small piece felt for nose template

1 reel extra-strong thread (to match fur fabric)

1 Follow instructions on pages 20–21 for making pattern templates and cutting out the materials.

2 Starting with one of the arms, pin a felt paw pad to the inner arm edge, tack in place and remove the pins. Thread a needle with some extra-strong thread and oversew the edges of the paw pad and the inner arm together along the seam line. Stitch the paw pad in place using a back stitch and finish off securely, then remove the tacking stitches and trim off any threads to neaten. Fold this part-sewn assembly in half with the fur sides together, pin together and tack, then remove the pins. Thread your needle with some more strong thread and oversew around the arm (Fig.1), leaving the opening for turning and jointing as marked on the pattern. Now stitch the arm securely together, using a reverse running stitch.

To do this, use the oversewing stitches as a guide and stitch around the arm with an ordinary running stitch (Fig.2). When you have reached the end of

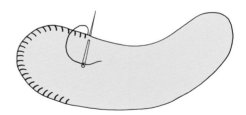

Fig.1 Oversew around the arm.

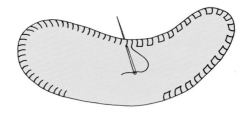

Fig.2 Using the oversewing stitches as a guide, stitch around the arm with an ordinary running stitch.

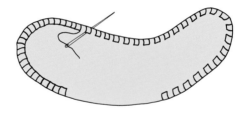

Fig.3 Reverse the direction of your stitching and fill in the gaps between your first running stitches.

the oversewing stitches, simply reverse the direction of your stitching and fill in the gaps between your first running stitches (Fig.3 page 58). Depending on the fabric used, you may find that because of the small size of the pieces some fraying of the fabric may make the final sewing of the closing seam a little difficult. An effective way to prevent this is to paint a p.v.a. water-soluble glue thinned 50/50 with water on to the very edges of the fabric backing and then allow it to dry while you wash the brush out in clean water. This is important as, like acrylic paint, while wet these glues are water-soluble but if the brushes are allowed to dry a new brush will be required! When the glued fabric is dry the glue line will be virtually transparent.

3 Now turn the arm fur side out, for which you will find that a small pair of forceps or seizers will be an invaluable aid. The second arm is made exactly as the first, the joints fitted and then they are stuffed in the normal way (see page 27) except that for this bear, kapok is the recommended stuffing.

4 The legs are dealt with in exactly the same way as the arms, using the same handsewing techniques and also the edge gluing on the fabric if required. You may find that due to the small size, it is impractical to pin the footpads so the best method for attaching these is to oversew the edges together to hold, after which the pads can be backstitched in place in the normal way.

5 The head is the usual three-piece design, made in the method described on pages 24–25, the only difference being the rather small size and the little extra patience that will be required. When sewn, the head is turned and finished off in the normal way. As with all of the teddy designs in this book, the ears, eyes and nose can be finished at this stage providing the head is stuffed and jointed (see pages 30–33).

6 The body is a simple two-piece body for which there is no necessity for darts and the make up is very straightforward. First, pin the two body pieces fur sides together the correct way up. Tack the pieces in place, remove all of the pins, oversew the edges and then backstitch. This part can be machine-sewn for those who wish but as the bear is so little, by the time your machine is threaded and ready the bear can probably be sewn quicker by

hand! Remove the tacking thread, trim off any loose ends and turn fur side out to complete the body.

7 Assembly of the bear is straightforward (see pages 28–29) and after all the joints have been checked, the bear is finally stuffed. It will be far easier to obtain a firm, evenly stuffed bear if you use kapok, but if it is unobtainable you could use polyester. However, to avoid bulk build-up, use only very small quantities at a time and ensure that it is firmly and evenly distributed in the bear.

8 The final grooming of the bear is now performed. If you used mohair, use a teasel brush or pin to lift any trapped pile from the seams. If you made your bear from velvet grooming will be unnecessary.

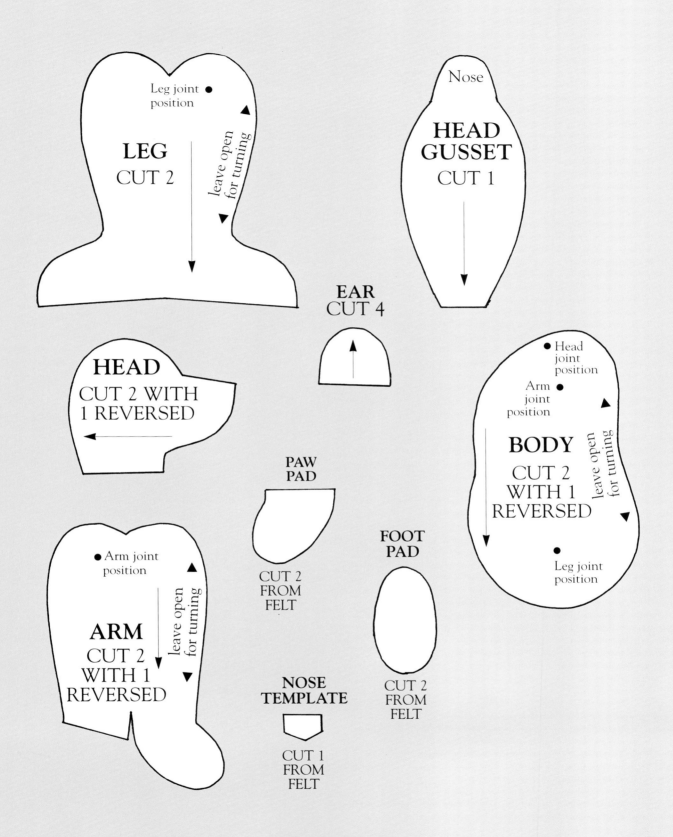

LEG
CUT 2

Leg joint position

leave open for turning

Nose

HEAD GUSSET
CUT 1

EAR
CUT 4

HEAD
CUT 2 WITH
1 REVERSED

PAW
PAD

CUT 2
FROM
FELT

Head joint position

Arm joint position

BODY
CUT 2
WITH 1
REVERSED

leave open for turning

Leg joint position

ARM
CUT 2
WITH 1
REVERSED

Arm joint position

leave open for turning

FOOT
PAD

CUT 2
FROM
FELT

NOSE
TEMPLATE

CUT 1
FROM
FELT

JASPER BEAR

SMUDGE

Smudge is the third of the miniature bears and, at only 3 inches (75mm) tall, the smallest! Although the prospect of making such a tiny fully-jointed teddy bear (pictured on page 59, top left) may appear daunting, he is in fact very simple and quick to make. Many people have found that making miniature teddy bears is relaxing and even addictive. This is probably because you can take a complete mini bear-making kit with you anywhere – as the sewing is by hand, all you need is the pre-cut fabric pieces, some thread and a needle and you will be able to make your teddies on a long train or car journey or while watching television. Although this bear is fully jointed, the design only uses one joint and that is for the head – the limbs are thread-jointed. It is probably easier to use the special mini bear fabric on a bear this small, as although it appears very similar to velvet on the outside it has a special backing bonded on to it to prevent fraying.

MATERIALS

10 x 10 inches (250 x 250mm) mini bear velvet fabric

1 x ¼ inch (7mm) fibreboard joint

2 x ¹⁄₁₆ inch (2mm) black beads for eyes

1 yd (91cm) black nose thread

1 oz (25g) kapok stuffing

2 x 2 inches (50 x 50mm) contrast velvet for pads

small piece black felt for nose template

1 reel extra-strong thread (to match fabric)

1 Follow the instructions on pages 20–21 for making your pattern templates and cutting out the materials.

2 This bear is made in exactly the same way as Jasper (see page 58), with the exception of the ears and the thread joints. Make the arms and legs in the usual way (see page 58), then turn and stuff them – as this bear is using thread joints you will find this step very quick because there are no joints to insert before stuffing. The seams on both arms and legs can all now be closed and the limbs placed to one side ready for assembly later.

3 As the ears are so tiny it would be impractical to use two pieces for this design. Each ear is simply made by folding one ear piece in half, pile sides together, and then oversewing and backstitching around the curved edge. The ear cannot now be turned, so the folded edge must be cut in a straight line along the base of the ear. Turn the ear through this cut opening and then oversew the edges, ready to attach to the head in the normal way.

4 Make up the head and body as for Jasper, remembering that this bear does have a joint in the head. When the head is complete with joint and stuffing, attach the eyes. For this small size, glass beads are a practical alternative to small glass looped eyes. Thread a needle with a double thickness of ordinary sewing cotton or invisible thread, then insert the needle at the back of the head at the base approximately in the centre line of the head gusset ensuring that the point of entry is as low down as possible to prevent the thread from being visible on the finished bear (Fig.1). Bring out the needle at the point where you wish the eye to be (Fig.2) and pull the thread through, leaving a small tail of thread at the point of entry. Pass your needle through the bead (Fig.3) and then reinsert the needle into the same hole from which it has just emerged (Fig.4) to exit adjacent to the thread tail. Remove the needle but do not cut any threads. You will now have two threads next to each other at the base of the head rear. Pull them tightly simultaneously to bring the eye into position, then

Fig.1 To attach the eyes, first insert the needle at the back of the head.

Fig.2 Bring out the needle at the point where the eye is to be.

7 Thread a needle with a double thickness of extra strong thread and pass it through an arm from one side to the other leaving a tail of thread approximately 2 inches (50mm) long (Fig.5). Reinsert the needle into the arm to emerge at the other side (Fig.6), having taken a ¼ inch (7mm) stitch, and then pass it through the locating hole in the body (Fig.7). Then thread the other arm on to the needle (Fig.8, page 64) and pass the needle back through the second arm (Fig.9, page 64) and through the body towards the first arm. Remove the needle from the thread (Fig.10) and knot the thread ends tightly and securely to the thread tail that was left outside the first arm in the initial stage.

Fig.3 Pass the needle through the bead.

Fig.4 Reinsert the needle into the same hole.

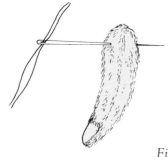

Fig.5 To make a thread joint, pass the needle through one arm.

knot the two threads together. Fit the second eye in the same way, using a point of entry as close as possible to the first.

5 The head is now attached to the body and the body is stuffed firmly, with the back seam finished off in the normal way with a ladder stitch. Only after this has been completed can you attach the arms and legs.

6 Thread joints are surprisingly strong and as long as you use a good quality extra-strong thread to attach them they should easily last the lifespan of the bear. First take the arms and pin them both on to the body to find the placing that suits you, then remove them after making a small mark on the body where they are to be jointed. Then take a very thick darning needle and, using it as a miniature awl, make a guiding hole, starting at one of the marks and passing right through the body to emerge at the second mark. When you remove the needle it will leave a fine locating hole through which the thread joints are installed.

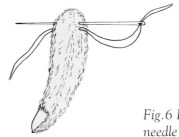

Fig.6 Reinsert the needle through the first arm.

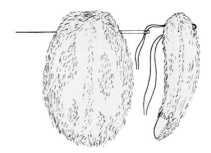

Fig.7 Pass the needle through the body.

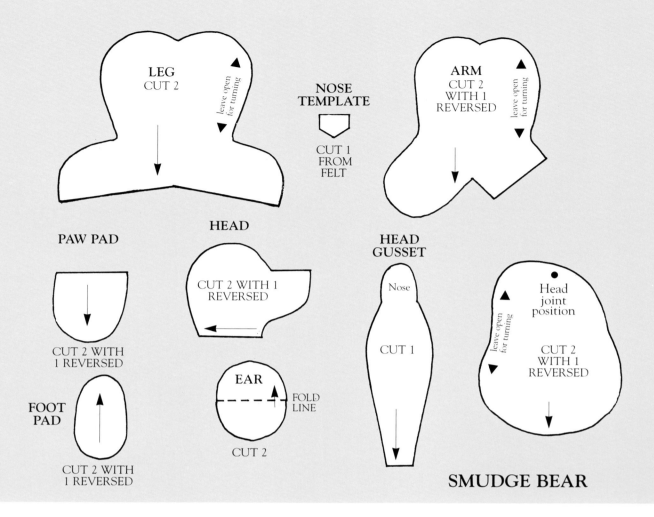

LEG
CUT 2

leave open for turning

NOSE TEMPLATE

CUT 1 FROM FELT

ARM
CUT 2 WITH 1 REVERSED

leave open for turning

PAW PAD

CUT 2 WITH 1 REVERSED

FOOT PAD

CUT 2 WITH 1 REVERSED

HEAD

CUT 2 WITH 1 REVERSED

EAR

FOLD LINE

CUT 2

HEAD GUSSET

Nose

CUT 1

Head joint position

leave open for turning

CUT 2 WITH 1 REVERSED

SMUDGE BEAR

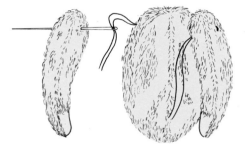

Fig.8 Thread the second arm on to the needle.

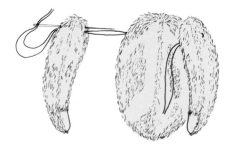

Fig.9 Reinsert the needle into the second arm and back through the body.

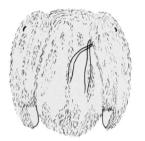

Fig.10 Remove the needle and knot the thread ends.

8 The legs are attached in the same manner as described for the arms, ensuring that all thread ends are neat and securely finished off. The only remaining feature on this bear is the embroidering of the nose and this procedure is as described on pages 31–32.

ALONZO BEAR

This teddy bear stands 12 inches (305mm) tall, is fully jointed and has many individual features, including pellet filling and sparse mohair. This mohair has a very thin pile where the backing is clearly visible and is intended to give the teddy bears an old look which can be further enhanced if you wish. Although the two bears shown on page 66 are from the same pattern, they do look a little different to each other. This is because we have given the darker bear an 'aged' look to give the illusion that he is considerably older than he is. This ageing takes the form of worn areas of fur, patches, obvious repairs and a general distressed look to the finished teddy. This ageing effect has become quite popular and is used on many of the ready-made artists' bears seen for sale.

MATERIALS

¼yd (25cm) ⅝ inch (15mm) sparse pile mohair

5 x 1½ inch (36mm) wooden joints

5½ yd (5m) black nose thread

½lb (250g) polyester stuffing

½lb (250g) plastic pellets

6 x 12 inches (150 x 300mm) wool mix felt for pads

1 reel sewing thread (to match fur fabric)

1 reel extra-strong thread (to match fur fabric)

1 pair ⅜ inch (9mm) genuine boot-button eyes or black glass eyes

1 sheet 600 grade wet and dry emery paper

small jar clear varnish (satin finish)

white spirit for thinning varnish

1 Follow the instructions on pages 20–21 for making your pattern templates and cutting out the materials.

2 The complete bear is very straightforward, being of the four-piece body type with a three-piece head, and he is sewn as described on pages 21–25.

3 Before stuffing any of the limbs you must decide if you want to include the plastic pellets in the limbs as well as the body. The pellets will add considerable weight to the finished bear and give

the characteristic 'sag' to the tummy. If you wish to use them in the arms and legs, you must first install the joints and firm a quantity of polyester stuffing around the joints and paws in the usual way, then add a small quantity of the pellets to the middle section between the polyester. Finally, add a thin covering layer of polyester stuffing before you close the seam. This is important as it will ensure that the pellets stay in position and will make the closing of the final seams with the ladder stitch that much easier to accomplish.

4 The head is stuffed with polyester in the normal way (see pages 25–26) – don't put pellets in it as the head has to be firmly stuffed for you to be able to embroider the nose and fit the glass eyes, and for it to retain its shape throughout the lifespan of the bear.

5 After the bear is assembled with the limbs and head attached (see pages 28–29), stuff it in the neck and shoulder area only with polyester stuffing, using just enough to ensure support for the arms and head. Fill the rest of the cavity with pellets. To judge the amount you need as you go, put a temporary thin layer of polyester stuffing into the final seam opening to prevent the pellets from spilling out and sit the bear down to see how he looks. Keep adding or taking away small amounts of pellets until you are satisfied, then lay the bear face down on a flat surface, place a final covering of polyester stuffing on top of the pellets to keep them stable and close the final seam with ladder stitch.

6 Authentic boot-button eyes are best for this teddy bear, but as these are quite difficult to obtain you may have to use 'antiqued' glass eyes instead. Take a pair of black glass eyes and sand them all over with the emery paper to roughen their shiny surface and give them a 'key' to receive a sealing coat of varnish diluted with an equal quantity of white spirit. As they dry, the eyes will take on a deep non-glossy sheen that will look convincingly like the genuine boot buttons. Allow them to dry overnight before attaching them (see pages 32–33).

7 The bear is now complete, but if you want to 'age' him you can do some further work to suit your taste. First, an old teddy bear will have some worn patches of fur, usually on the head, arm and chest areas. To simulate this, you can shave the fur with a small pair of pointed scissors. Snip the pile away gradually until you achieve the effect you want, always cutting in the direction of the pile and never across it to make it look as natural as possible.

8 The next option is the addition of one or two felt patches. Don't try to obtain a perfect colour match and don't stitch them on too unobtrusively – they should be noticeable without being too glaringly so. For maximum effect, put them at points of obvious wear only and don't be tempted to add more.

9 Teddy bears that have seen a lot of use often have a repair to a seam. Use an over-thick thread or wool in a slightly prominent colour and take uneven stitches to give the effect of a rushed repair.

10 General discoloration of the sort that comes with age is especially important if your teddy bear has been made from one of the lighter shades of mohair. The most convincing way to simulate this is to sharpen a soft pencil into a saucer and remove the wood shavings to leave the pencil graphite, which can be crushed into a fine powder with the bowl of a spoon. With your fingertip, apply the graphite dust in very small amounts to the area you wish to discolour, rubbing it in gently in small circular movements and gradually increasing them in size to blend in the discoloration with the surrounding area. It is a good idea to practice this technique first on a piece of white cloth.

11 Finally, the nose. Over the years, the embroidered nose of an old bear will have become unravelled and a repair will have been made. Simulate this by embroidering the nose slightly unevenly, with irregular gaps in the threads – as with all of the ageing processes described, you should not exaggerate the effect as it will look less convincing. Your bear should now look like a real old teddy that has been passed from generation to generation.

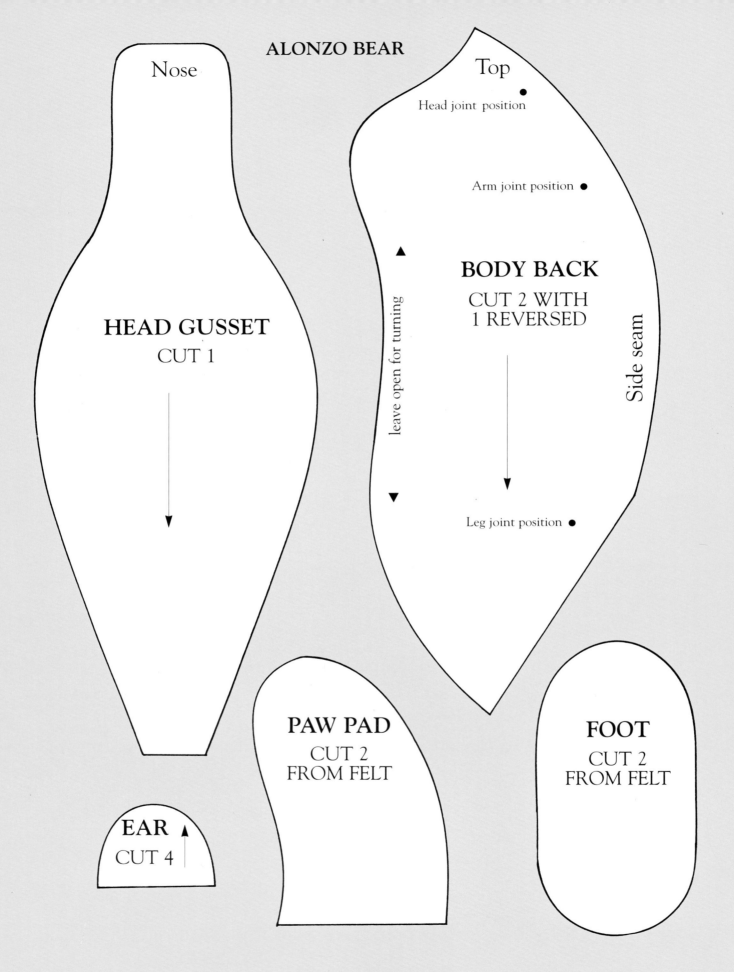

ALONZO BEAR

Nose

HEAD GUSSET
CUT 1

Top

Head joint position

Arm joint position

BODY BACK
CUT 2 WITH
1 REVERSED

leave open for turning

Side seam

Leg joint position

PAW PAD
CUT 2
FROM FELT

FOOT
CUT 2
FROM FELT

EAR
CUT 4

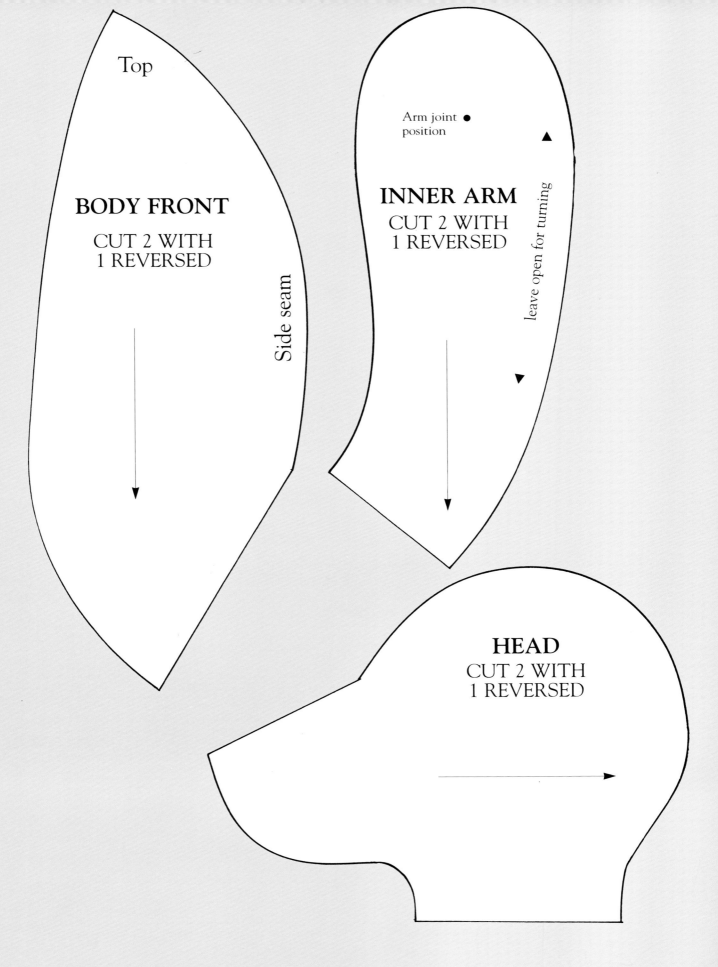

Top

BODY FRONT

CUT 2 WITH
1 REVERSED

Side seam

Arm joint ● position

INNER ARM

CUT 2 WITH
1 REVERSED

leave open for turning

HEAD

CUT 2 WITH
1 REVERSED

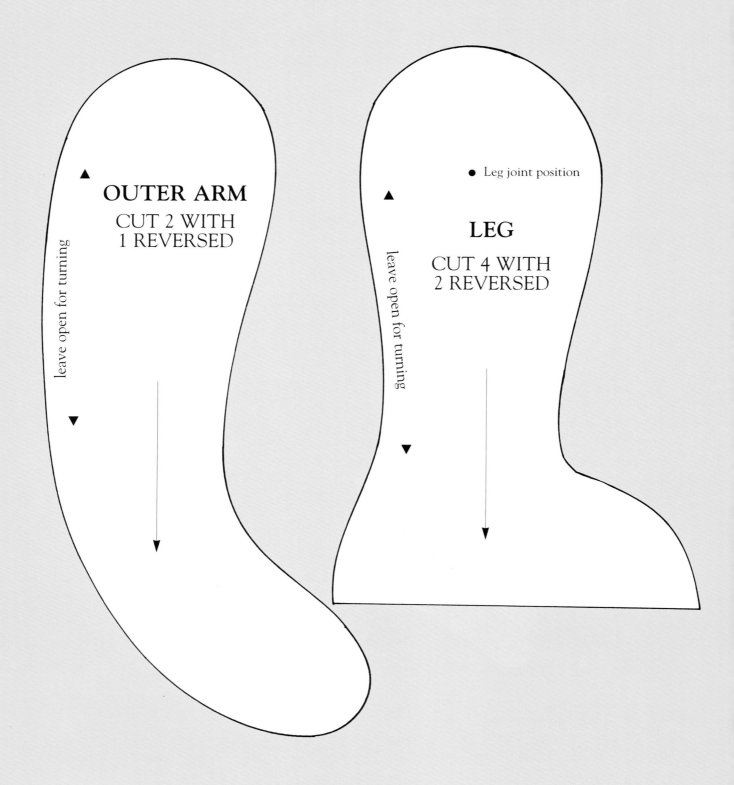

OUTER ARM

CUT 2 WITH
1 REVERSED

leave open for turning

● Leg joint position

LEG

CUT 4 WITH
2 REVERSED

leave open for turning

ALONZO BEAR

OLIVER BEAR

T his 16 inch (400mm) teddy bear (shown on page 73) is the first of the two dressed teddy bears featured in this book. He is simple to make and is dressed in a velvet suit with a lace-edged shirt. If you do not feel confident about making buttonholes you can substitute Velcro or dress fasteners and sew false buttons on the front of the shirt for effect.

MATERIALS

½ yd (45cm) ⅜ inch (8mm) distressed pile mohair

5 x 2 inch (50mm) wooden joints

1 pair ½ inch (12mm) amber glass eyes

5½ yd (5m) black nose thread

1½ lb (750g) polyester stuffing

6 x 12 inches (150 x 300mm) wool mix felt for pads

small piece black felt for nose template

1 reel sewing thread (to match fur fabric)

1 reel extra-strong thread (to match fur fabric)

FOR THE CLOTHES

½ yd (45cm) velvet

¼ yd (25cm) white cotton

3 x ⅜ inch (10mm) buttons

1 yd (91cm) 2 inch (50mm) wide scalloped edge lace

15 inches (380mm) ½ inch (12mm) elastic

sewing thread to match

1 First make the bear following the instructions on pages 20–33, then make the clothes in the following sequence, using a ¼ inch (7mm) seam allowance throughout. Many of the pattern pieces are cut on the fold, and if you are using a pile fabric such as velvet it is important that the pattern pieces are first cut out from paper, again on the fold. After the paper pattern has been unfolded, it is then used to cut out the actual fabric piece. If you have chosen a simple cotton print fabric this procedure will not be necessary, although you may find it quite useful.

Stitching the shirt fronts to the shirt back.

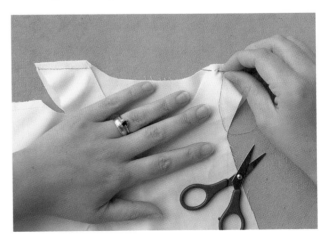

Attaching the back shirt facing.

2 First make the shirt by stitching the shirt fronts to the shirt back at the shoulder and side seams, ensuring that the attached front facings are not folded back and caught in the shoulder seam. Next attach the back facing to the front facing along the shoulder seam and stitch in place.

3 Tack the lace collar in place along the neck edge of the shirt, placing the edges of the lace on the fold line of the front facing. Then fold the front facing to the outside along the fold line and stitch both front and back facings into place along the neck edge, right sides together. This procedure will also serve to secure the collar in place.

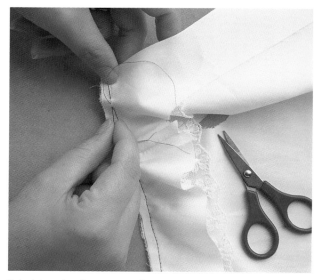

Stitching the facings in place.

4 To make the sleeves, stitch the lace cuff to the bottom of each sleeve then fold the sleeve in half, right sides together, and stitch along the straight edge, making the underarm seam. Insert the sleeves into the armholes and stitch in place. Finally, hem the shirt and add three buttons and buttonholes.

5 The jacket is made in a similar manner to the shirt, except that the front facings are separate and there is no collar. First stitch the back facings to the front facings at the shoulder seams, then, after you have stitched the front jacket pieces to the back at the shoulder and side seams, attach the facings to the jacket right sides together and stitch in place around their entire edges. Hem the bottom edge and then topstitch around the whole jacket to hold all the facings to the inside. Make up the sleeves and insert them into the jacket in the same way as for the shirt.

6 To make the trousers, place the two trouser pieces right sides together and stitch along the two curved seams as in the diagram. Bring these completed seams together and sew around the

Assembling the trousers.

remaining seam to make the inside legs. Next make the casing for the elastic in the waistband, thread the elastic through and stitch the ends together. Finally, make the trouser cuffs by hemming the bottom edges and then folding each cuff in half right sides together and stitching along the short edge. Gather the trouser legs slightly at the bottom and stitch on the cuffs.

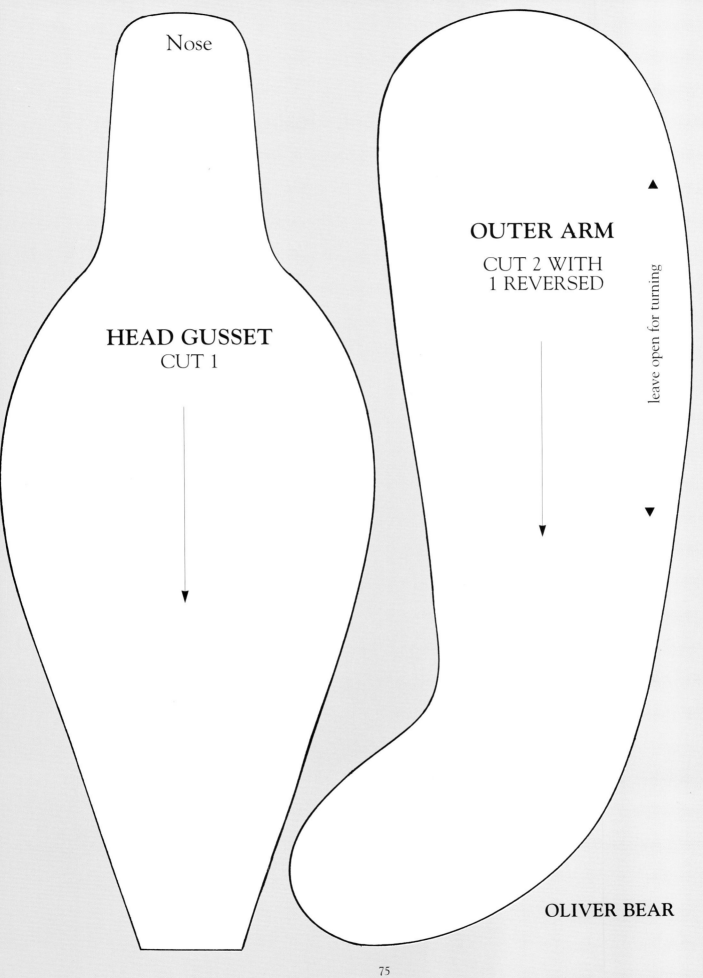

Nose

HEAD GUSSET
CUT 1

OUTER ARM

CUT 2 WITH
1 REVERSED

leave open for turning

Nose

OLIVER BEAR

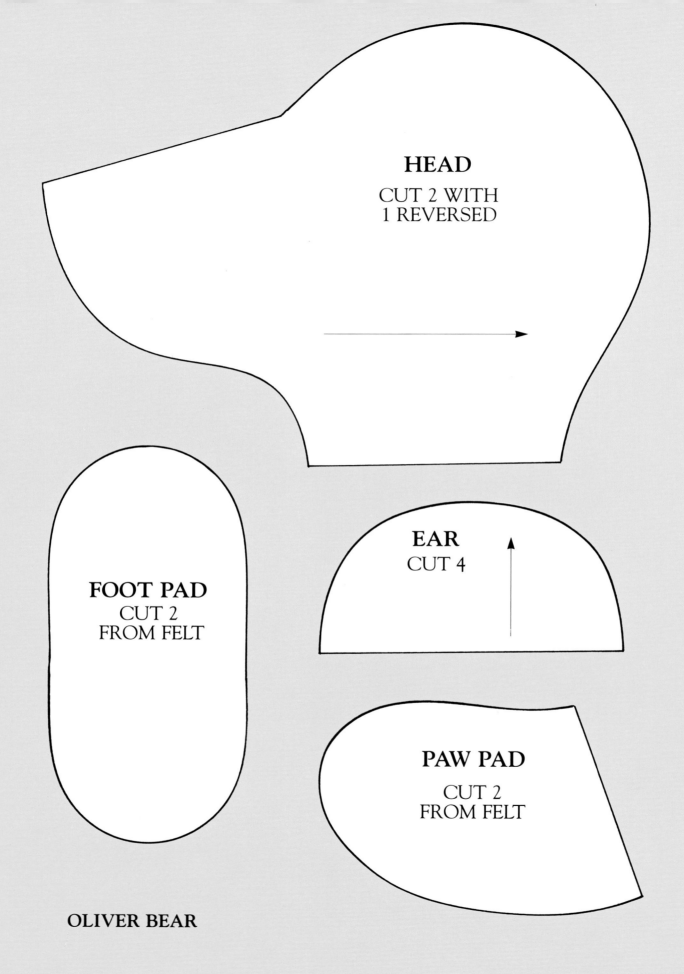

HEAD
CUT 2 WITH
1 REVERSED

EAR
CUT 4

FOOT PAD
CUT 2
FROM FELT

PAW PAD
CUT 2
FROM FELT

OLIVER BEAR

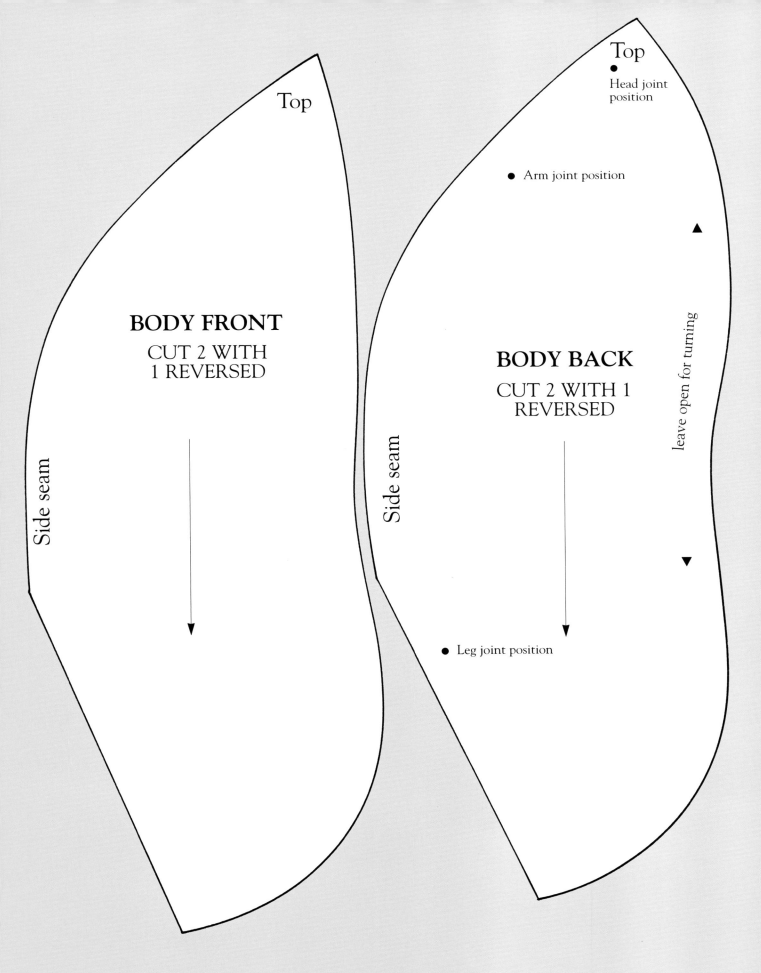

BODY FRONT

CUT 2 WITH
1 REVERSED

Side seam

Top

BODY BACK

CUT 2 WITH 1
REVERSED

Top

Head joint
position

Arm joint position

leave open for turning

Side seam

Leg joint position

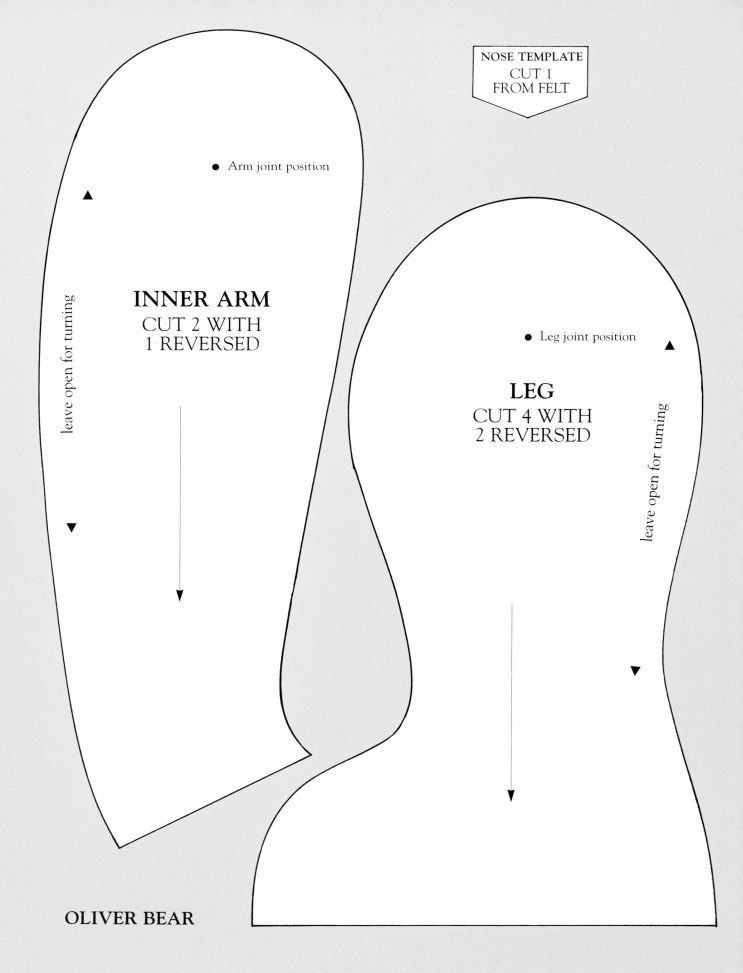

NOSE TEMPLATE
CUT 1
FROM FELT

• Arm joint position

INNER ARM
CUT 2 WITH
1 REVERSED

leave open for turning

• Leg joint position

LEG
CUT 4 WITH
2 REVERSED

leave open for turning

OLIVER BEAR

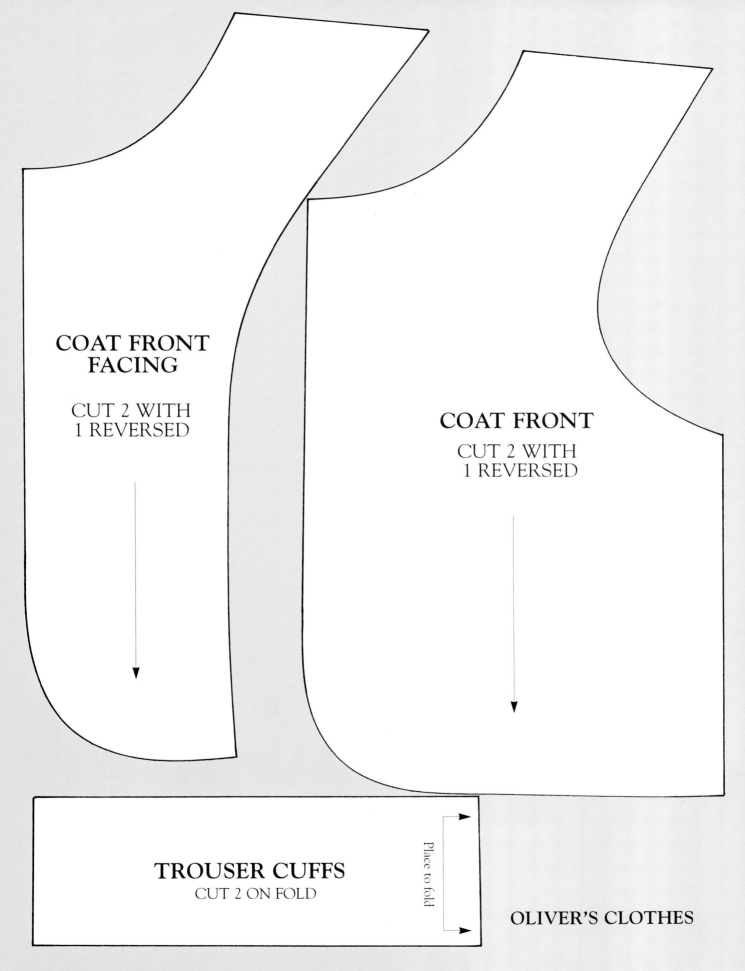

**COAT FRONT
FACING**

CUT 2 WITH
1 REVERSED

COAT FRONT

CUT 2 WITH
1 REVERSED

TROUSER CUFFS
CUT 2 ON FOLD

Place to fold

OLIVER'S CLOTHES

Place to fold

COAT SLEEVE
CUT 2 ON FOLD

SHIRT BACK
CUT 1 ON FOLD

Place to fold

OLIVER'S CLOTHES

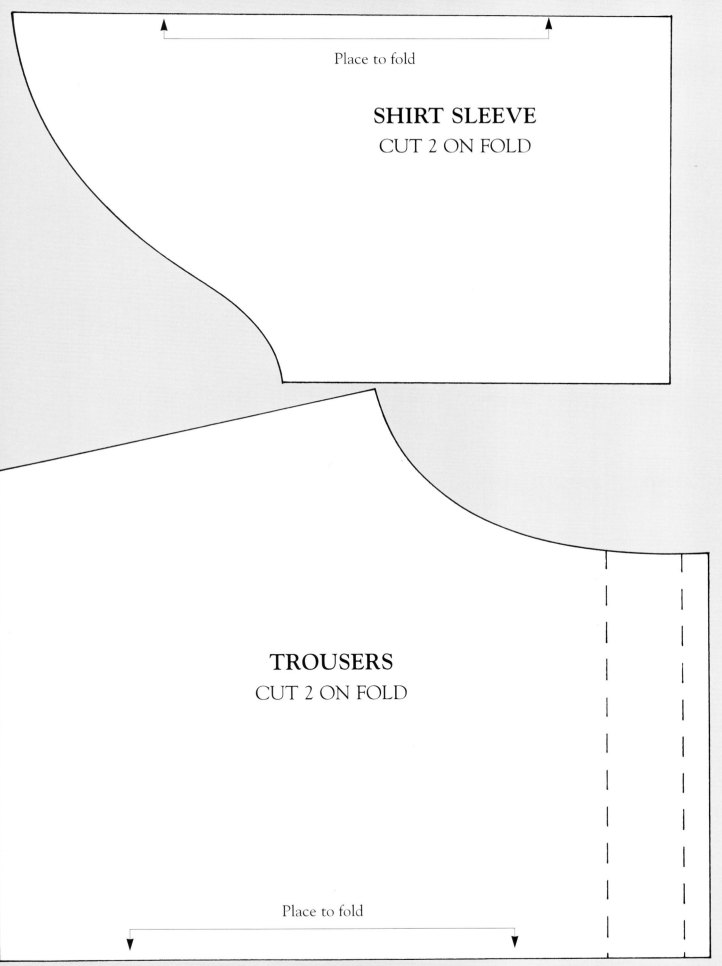

Place to fold

SHIRT SLEEVE
CUT 2 ON FOLD

TROUSERS
CUT 2 ON FOLD

Place to fold

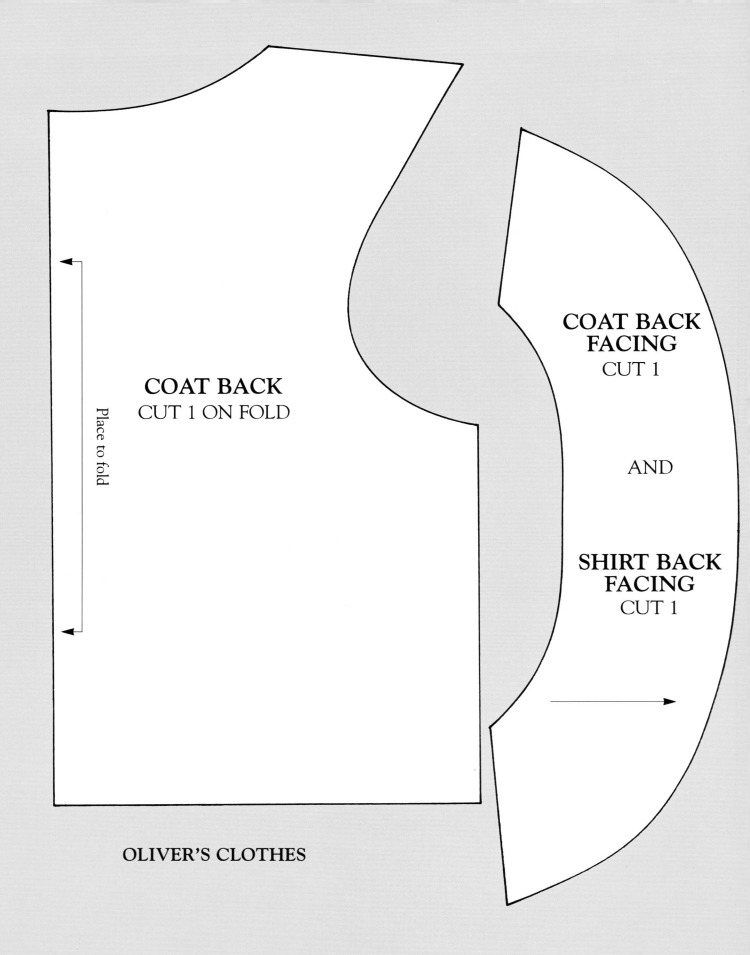

COAT BACK
CUT 1 ON FOLD

Place to fold

COAT BACK
FACING
CUT 1

AND

SHIRT BACK
FACING
CUT 1

OLIVER'S CLOTHES

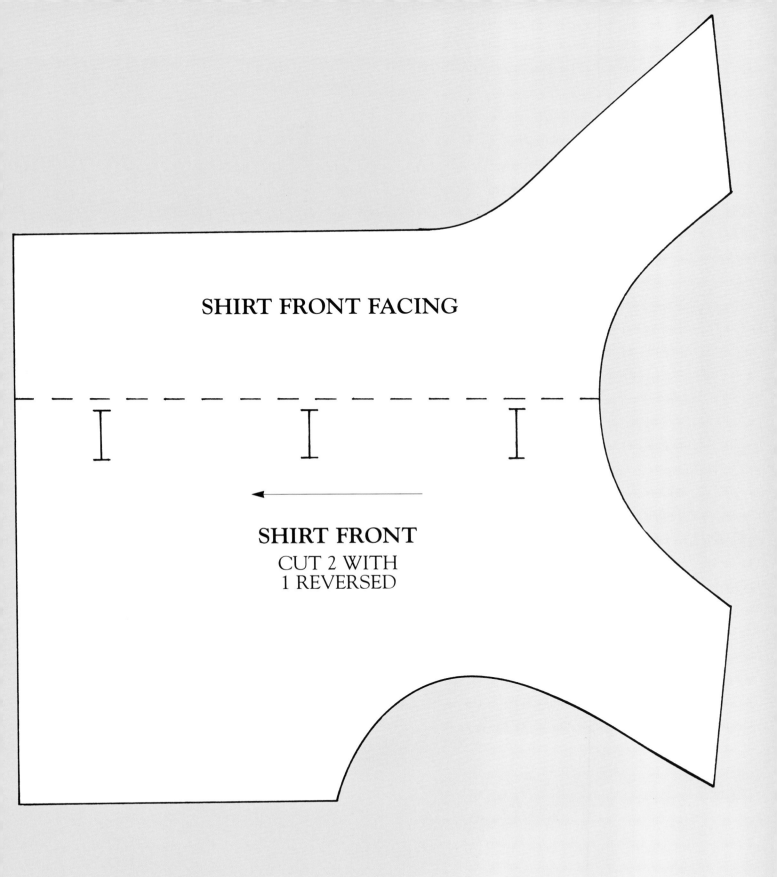

SHIRT FRONT FACING

SHIRT FRONT
CUT 2 WITH
1 REVERSED

ADDITIONAL CLOTHES FOR OLIVER

An alternative outfit for Oliver will enable him to be dressed ready for bedtime in a pair of striped pyjamas along with a traditional dressing gown. The pyjamas are a miniature version of full-sized ones, right down to the buttonholes and draw cord. The pattern can also be used for Olivia for a further outfit. Olivia's set of additional clothes (see page 100) – a smart school uniform of blazer, blouse and skirt – can also be modified to create an extra outfit for Oliver. The blazer and shirt are the same while the skirt is simply replaced with a pair of trousers. To do this, follow the basic pattern and instructions for making the pyjamas on page 84 – 88, substituting a suitable grey material. For the waist simply omit the pyjama draw cord and use elastic instead.

MATERIALS

½ yd x 54 inches (45 x 140cm) of cotton stripe-print fabric for the pyjamas

½ yd x 54 inches (45 x 140cm) of wool tartan fabric or similar for the dressing gown

3 x ½ inch (12mm) buttons

¾ yd (75cm) of cotton piping cord

sewing threads to match

1 First trace all the pattern pieces onto the respective fabrics and cut them all out. Use a ¼ inch (7mm) seam allowance for all stitching. Start with the pyjama fronts which are pinned to the pyjama back right sides together and sewn at both shoulder and side seams.

2 Make the sleeves by folding each sleeve piece in half right sides together and stitch the underarm seam. Turn right sides out and stitch into the pyjama armholes right sides together. Neatly hem the pyjama jacket and repeat for the sleeves. Press under ⅝ inch (15mm) along the front edges of the jacket and stitch in place.

3 Sew the two collar pieces right sides together leaving the bottom edge open. Turn right side out and lightly press under the seam allowance along one edge. Sew the collar right sides together to the neck edge of the jacket keeping the pressed edge free. Press the completed collar flat so that the pressed straight edge of the collar can be slip stitched onto the inside of the jacket to enclose the seam. Finally make three buttonholes where indicated and sew on three buttons.

4 The trousers are a simple two-piece design with a draw cord. First, place the two trouser pieces right sides together and sew along the curved edges only. Line up the completed seams, lightly press and sew the remaining seam to make the inside leg. Hem the legs and finally make the casing for the draw cord by turning the top edge of the completed trousers and stitching in place, leaving a sufficient gap to insert your draw cord. Attach the cord to a safety pin and thread through the completed trousers to finish.

5 To make the dressing gown, sew the two gown fronts to the back at the shoulder and side seams right sides together. As with the pyjamas, fold each sleeve right sides together and sew the underarm seam before inserting the completed sleeve into the armholes. Hem the sleeves.

6 Sew the two collar pieces together at the centre back seam, then attach the completed collar to the gown matching points A, B and C as indicated on the pattern. Press flat then sew the gown collar facings together to the gown front matching at points A, C and D. Fold to the inside and press, slip stitch in place if required and then hem the bottom of the gown.

7 To make the belt loops press all the seam allowances to the inside and stitch in place onto the gown approximately ¾ inch (20mm) under the arms on each side seam. Make the pockets in the same way but remember to turn and press the top edge to neaten. Stitch the pockets in place. Finally the belt is folded in half along its length and sewn leaving a small gap in the centre for turning. Turn and press the belt and slip stitch the opening. Pass the belt through the belt loops to finish.

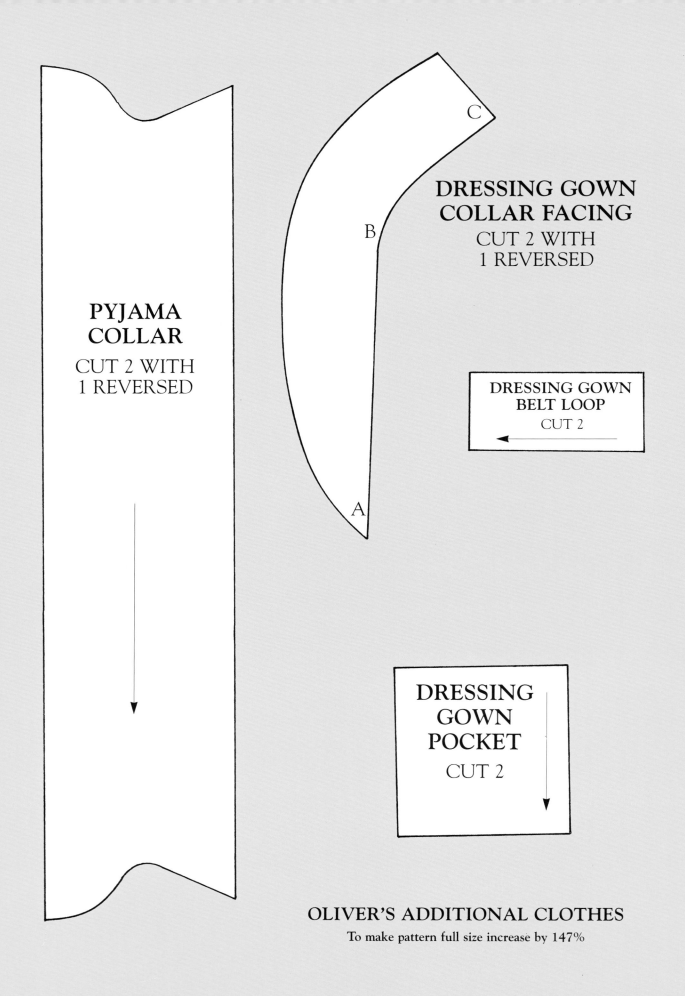

PYJAMA COLLAR

CUT 2 WITH
1 REVERSED

DRESSING GOWN COLLAR FACING

CUT 2 WITH
1 REVERSED

C

B

A

DRESSING GOWN
BELT LOOP

CUT 2

DRESSING GOWN POCKET

CUT 2

OLIVER'S ADDITIONAL CLOTHES

To make pattern full size increase by 147%

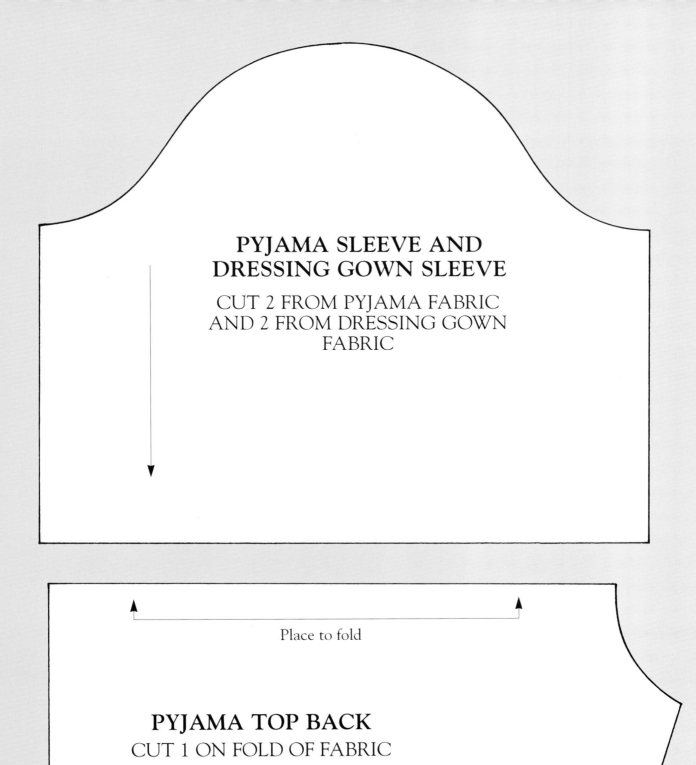

**PYJAMA SLEEVE AND
DRESSING GOWN SLEEVE**

CUT 2 FROM PYJAMA FABRIC
AND 2 FROM DRESSING GOWN
FABRIC

Place to fold

PYJAMA TOP BACK
CUT 1 ON FOLD OF FABRIC

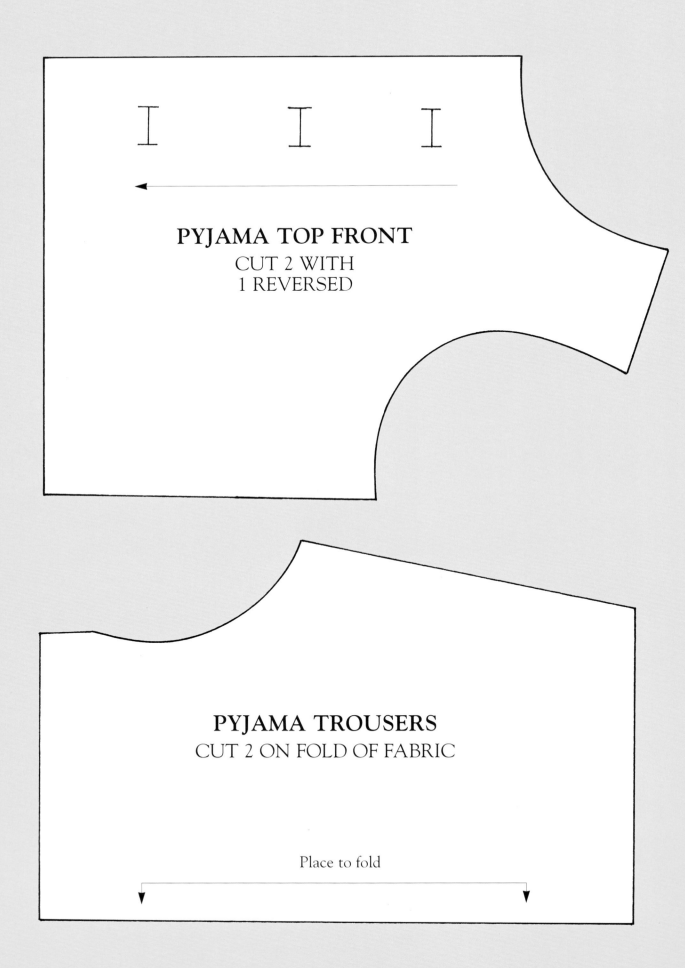

PYJAMA TOP FRONT

CUT 2 WITH
1 REVERSED

PYJAMA TROUSERS

CUT 2 ON FOLD OF FABRIC

Place to fold

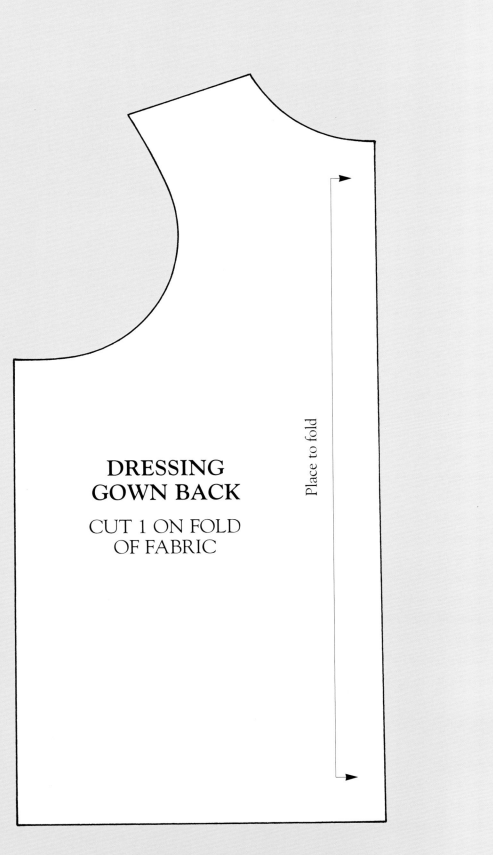

DRESSING GOWN BACK

CUT 1 ON FOLD
OF FABRIC

Place to fold

DRESSING GOWN BELT

CUT 1 ON
FOLD
OF FABRIC

Place to fold

OLIVER'S ADDITIONAL CLOTHES

To make pattern full size increase by 147%

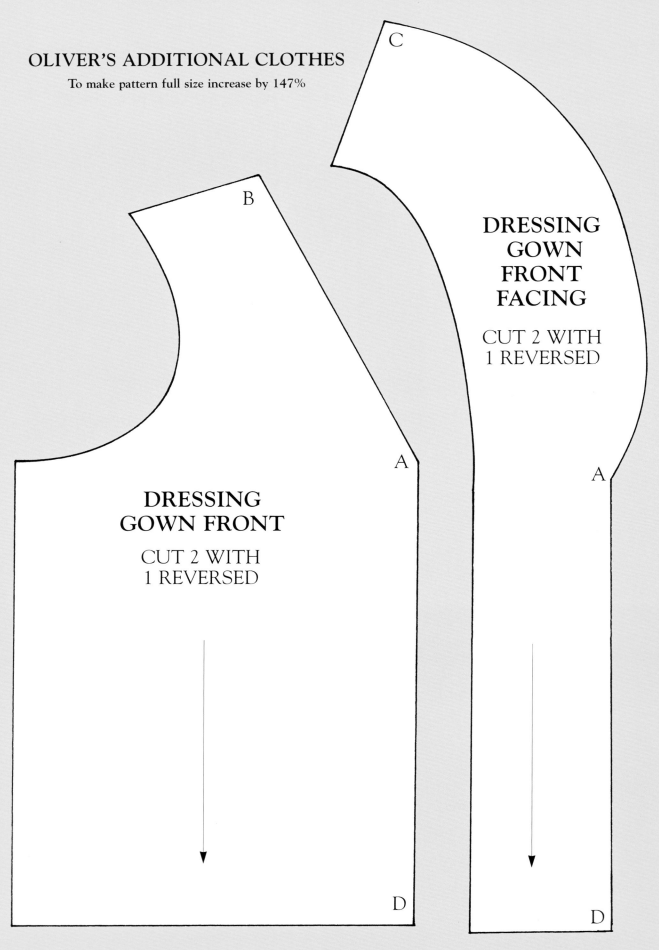

OLIVER'S ADDITIONAL CLOTHES
To make pattern full size increase by 147%

C

B

**DRESSING
GOWN
FRONT
FACING**

CUT 2 WITH
1 REVERSED

A

**DRESSING
GOWN FRONT**

CUT 2 WITH
1 REVERSED

A

D

D

OLIVIA BEAR

This 15 inch (385mm) bear (pictured on page 72) is the companion to Oliver. Like him, she is traditional in style but has been designed without the hump to allow the fitting of the clothes. Here she is wearing a navy blue dress that features a dropped waist with a pleated skirt, a lace-edged puritan collar and white-edged sleeves, giving her a smart appearance. However, you could change the fabric to give her a very different aspect – perhaps a fresh floral design to make her into a country-girl bear. If you do choose a patterned fabric, make sure the design is a small one so she is not overwhelmed by it.

MATERIALS

½ yd (45cm) ⅜ inch (8mm) distressed pile mohair

5 x 2 inch (50mm) wooden joints

1 pair ½ inch (12mm) amber glass eyes

5½ yd (5m) black nose thread

1½ lb (750g) polyester stuffing

6 x 12 inches (150 x 300mm) wool mix felt for pads

small piece black felt for nose template

1 reel sewing thread (to match fur fabric)

1 reel extra-strong thread (to match fur fabric)

FOR THE CLOTHES

½ yd (45cm) navy blue cotton fabric

½ yd (45cm) ½ inch (12mm) white bias binding

⅔ yd (60cm) ⅜ inch (10mm) white lace

3 x ½ inch (12mm) buttons

sewing thread to match

1 First make the bear following the instructions on pages 20–33. Then proceed to make the clothes. Cut out all of the pattern pieces from your chosen material. There is no pattern piece for the skirt as this is simply a rectangle of fabric measuring 42 x 5 inches (106 x 12cm). When stitching, use a ¼ inch (7mm) seam allowance throughout.

2 To make the collar, tack your lace edging around the curved edge on one collar piece on the right side directly on top of the stitching line. Pin and tack the second collar piece on to the first, right sides together, and with the tacking from the lace edging uppermost, stitch the collar pieces together following this tacking line exactly. Turn the collar right sides out and you will see that the lace forms an attractive edging to the collar.

The lace edging tacked to the stitching line of the dress collar.

3 To make the dress bodice, stitch the back facing to the front facings right sides together at the shoulder seam. Stitch the front dress bodice pieces to the back bodice piece at the shoulder and side seams then tack the collar to the bodice along the neck edge, lining up the lace edging to the stitching

line on the front opening. Next place the facings on the dress bodice, matching the shoulder seams and the front openings, and stitch in place around the entire edge, which will secure the collar in place.

4 The sleeves are made next. First stitch the white bias binding in place along the bottom edge of each sleeve, then fold the sleeve in half and stitch along the straight edge to form the underarm seam. Turn the sleeves right side out and then insert into the armholes of the bodice and stitch to secure.

5 Make the three buttonholes on the bodice as marked on the pattern, sew on the buttons and then button up the bodice. At this point, where the front edges overlap at the bottom edge, tack to hold in place ready to attach the skirt.

The skirt pleating.

6 Now make the pleated skirt from the rectangle of fabric. You will probably find it easier to hem the skirt first along one of the long edges. To make the pleats, using a ruler and tailor's chalk, simply mark equal spaces of exactly ¾ inch (2cm) along the entire length of the material, marking both top and bottom as you proceed. Take a small straight edge and then, using tailor's chalk, connect the first top mark to the first bottom mark with a dotted line. Connect the second top and bottom mark with a straight solid line and the third top and bottom mark with a dotted line as the first. You will now

have a section of three chalk connections, one dotted, one straight and another dotted, and this will make up one complete pleat. Repeat this marking sequence across the whole width of the fabric, ending with a dotted line (see diagram).

7 To make the first pleat, fold the material right sides together along the first solid line, bringing together the dotted lines on either side of it. Lay the folded pleat flat and pin to secure at the top and bottom. Make up the second pleat in the same way and continue in this fashion across the entire width of the fabric. When all the pleats have been made, tack along the top and bottom edges to hold the pleats in place and remove all of the pins so that the pleats can be pressed into position, using a steam iron if possible.

8 Next fold the skirt in half, align the two short edges and stitch them together to form the back seam of the skirt. Stitch the skirt to the bodice and remove all the tacking stitches that were holding the pleats in place.

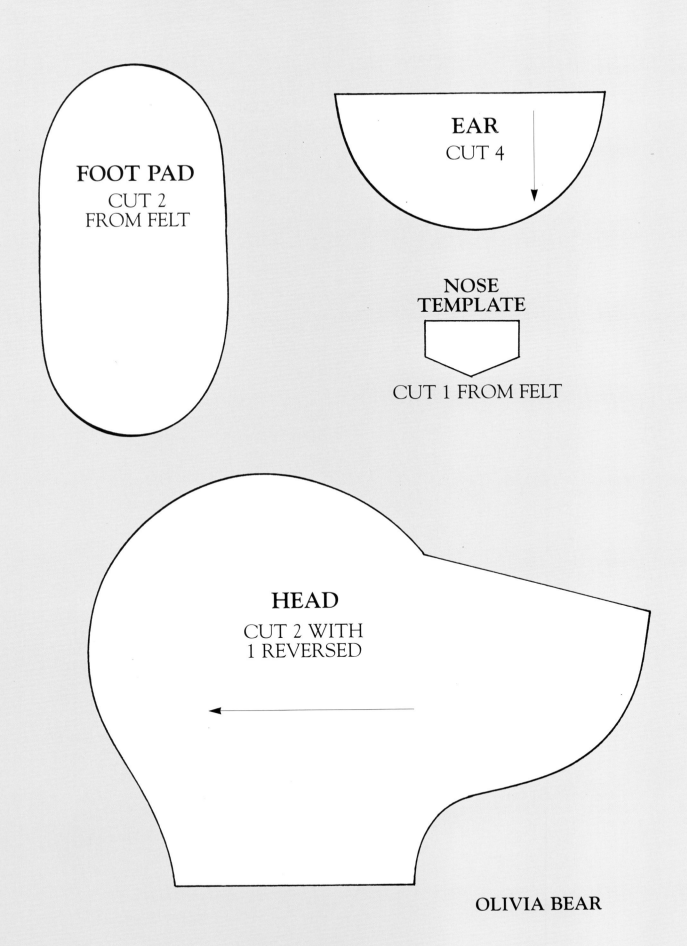

FOOT PAD
CUT 2
FROM FELT

EAR
CUT 4

**NOSE
TEMPLATE**

CUT 1 FROM FELT

HEAD
CUT 2 WITH
1 REVERSED

OLIVIA BEAR

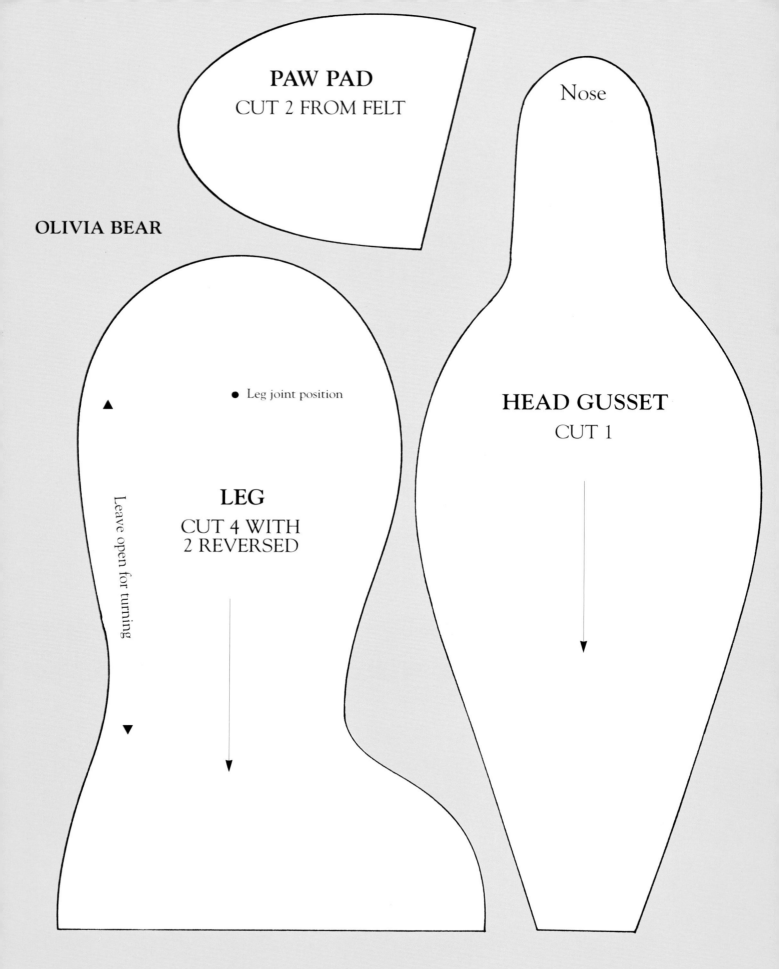

PAW PAD
CUT 2 FROM FELT

Nose

OLIVIA BEAR

● Leg joint position

HEAD GUSSET
CUT 1

Leave open for turning

LEG
CUT 4 WITH
2 REVERSED

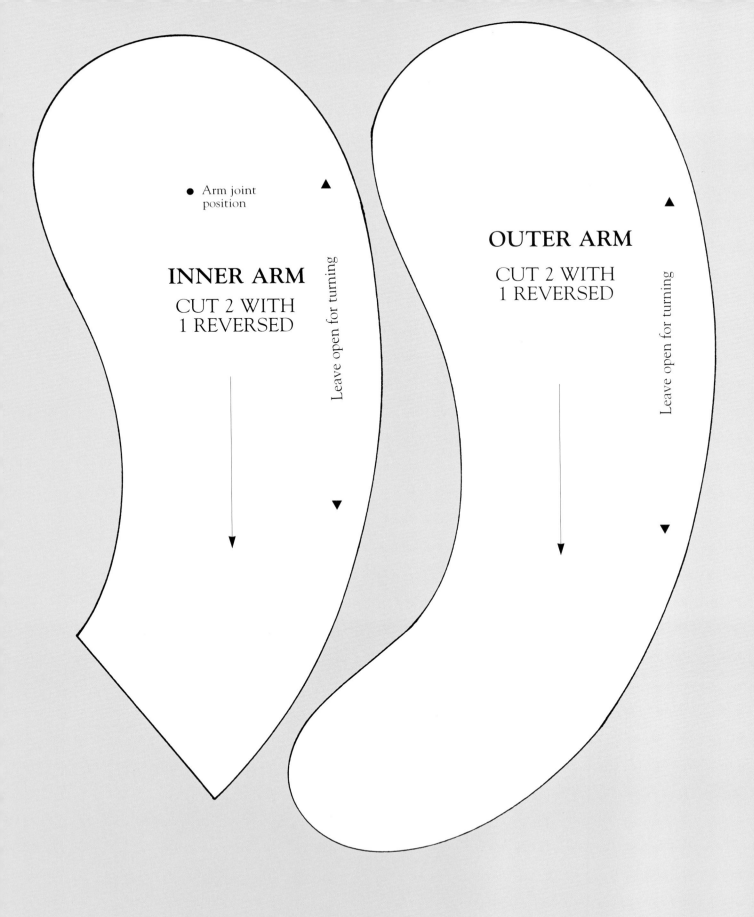

● Arm joint
position

INNER ARM

CUT 2 WITH
1 REVERSED

Leave open for turning

OUTER ARM

CUT 2 WITH
1 REVERSED

Leave open for turning

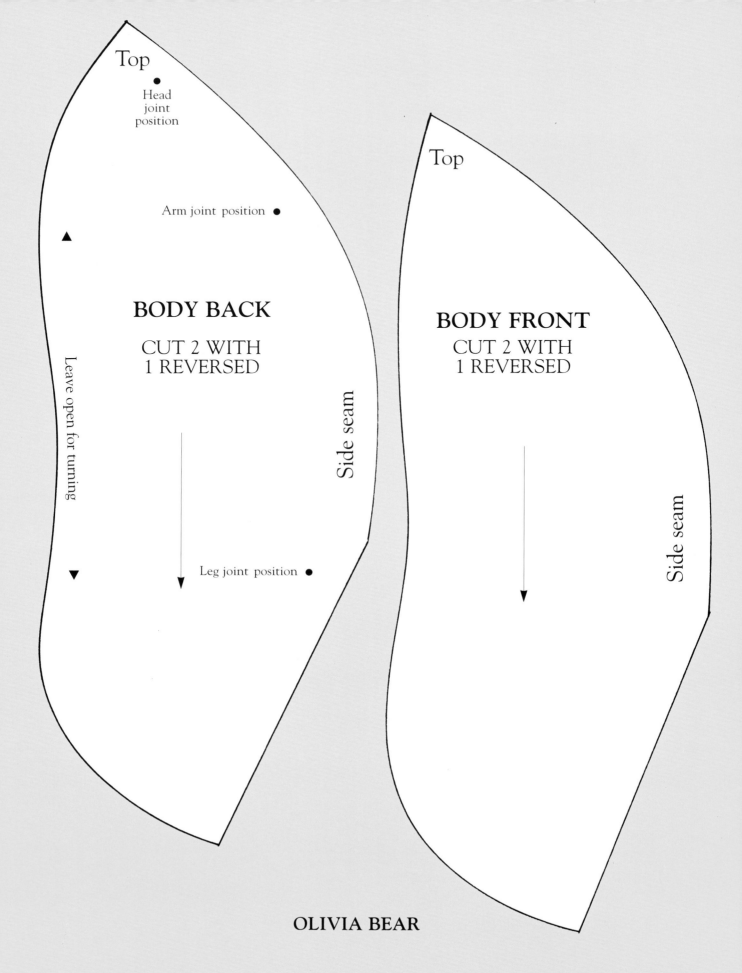

Top

Head
joint
position

Arm joint position ●

BODY BACK

**CUT 2 WITH
1 REVERSED**

Leave open for turning

Side seam

Leg joint position ●

Top

BODY FRONT

**CUT 2 WITH
1 REVERSED**

Side seam

OLIVIA BEAR

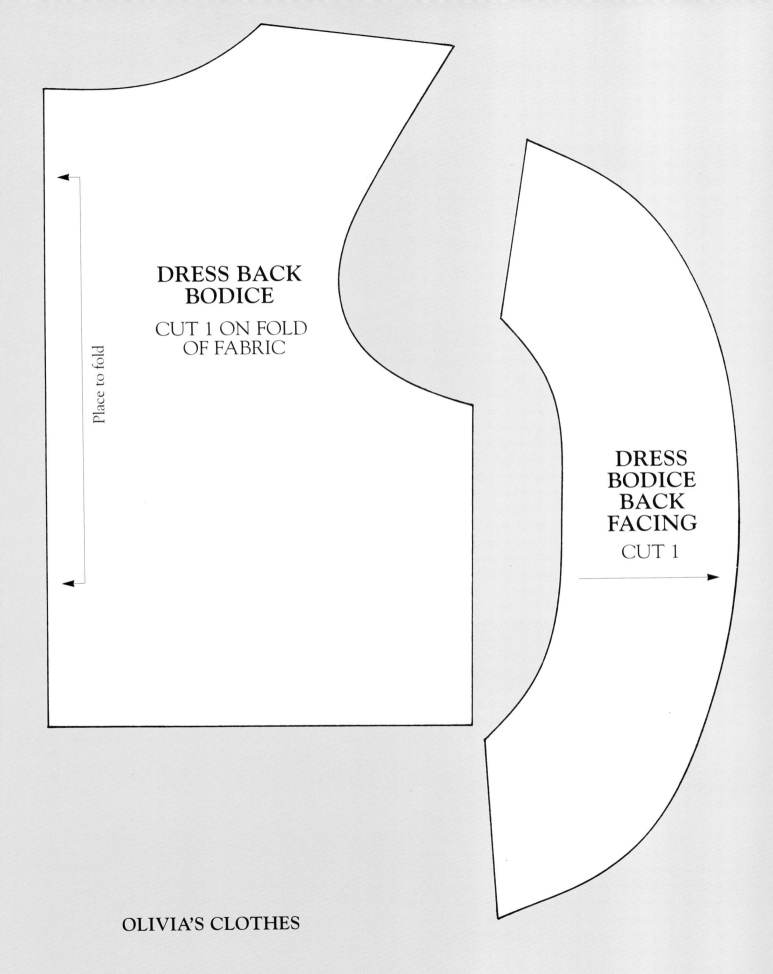

**DRESS BACK
BODICE**

CUT 1 ON FOLD
OF FABRIC

Place to fold

**DRESS
BODICE
BACK
FACING**

CUT 1

OLIVIA'S CLOTHES

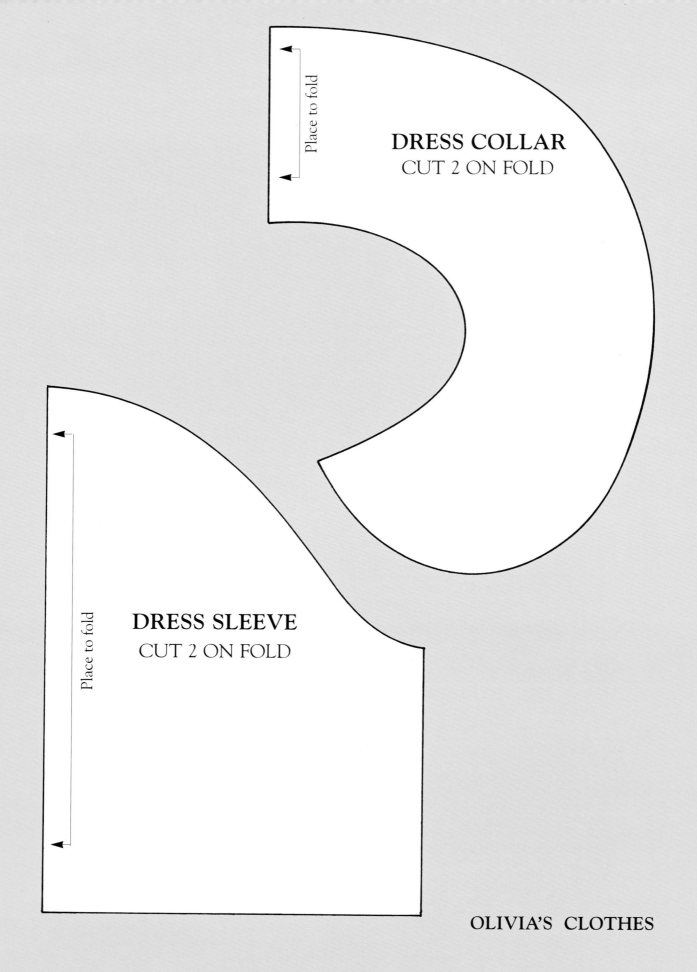

DRESS COLLAR
CUT 2 ON FOLD

Place to fold

DRESS SLEEVE
CUT 2 ON FOLD

Place to fold

OLIVIA'S CLOTHES

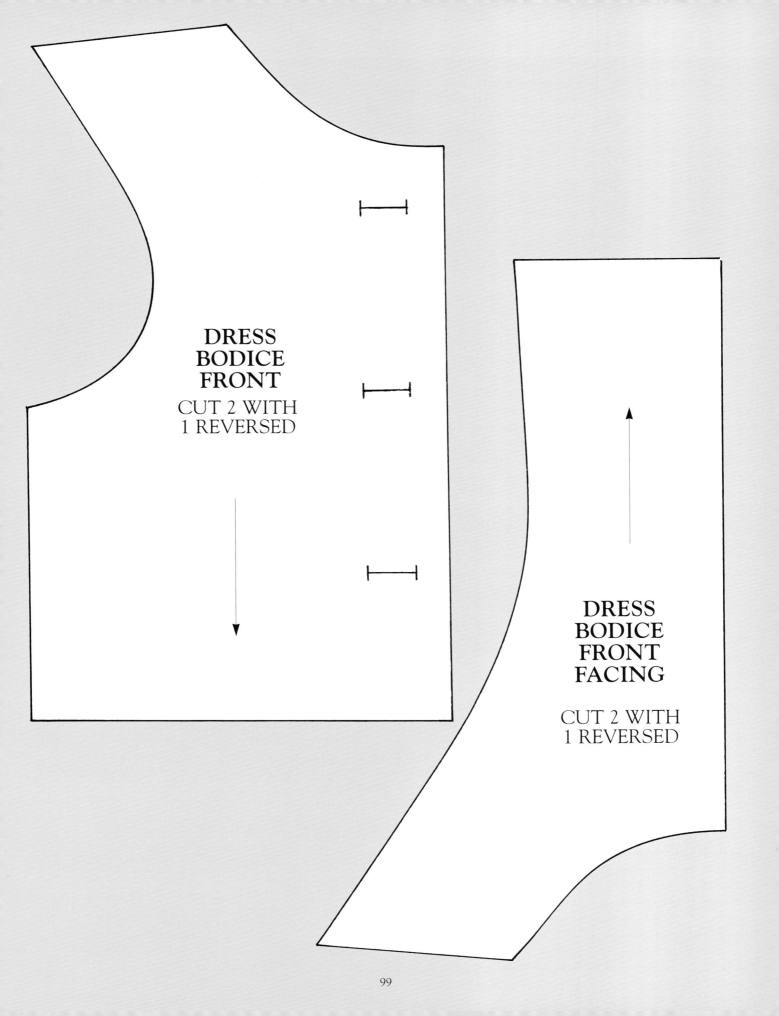

**DRESS
BODICE
FRONT**

CUT 2 WITH
1 REVERSED

**DRESS
BODICE
FRONT
FACING**

CUT 2 WITH
1 REVERSED

ADDITIONAL CLOTHES FOR OLIVIA

Olivia's second outfit has her ready for school in a smart blazer, blouse and skirt. This uniform can be made to suit a local school.

MATERIALS

¼ yd x 72 inches (25 x 185cm) of felt for the blazer in a suitable colour

72 inches (185cm) of ½ inch (12mm) bias binding to edge the blazer

1 x ¾ inch (20mm) button

¼ yd x 54 inches (25 x 140cm) white cotton fabric for the blouse

¼ yd x 54 inches (25 x 140cm) grey cotton fabric for skirt or trousers

8 inches (200mm) Velcro (hook and loop fastening) or three ¼ inch (7mm) buttons

10 inches (25cm) of ½ inch (12mm) wide elastic for the skirt waistband

1 small child's elasticated school tie and a cap badge (to use as a blazer badge) optional

sewing threads to match

1 Transfer the pattern pieces onto the various fabrics and cut them all out. Use a ¼ inch (7mm) seam allowance for all stitching.

2 Starting with the blazer, place the blazer fronts onto the blazer back and stitch together at the shoulder and side seams.

3 Next make the sleeves by folding each sleeve in half and stitching the underarm seam before inserting the completed sleeves into the respective armholes and stitching in place.

4 To make the collar, place the two collar pieces on top of each other and stitch together along the stitching line only, as shown on the pattern. Turn the collar right side out after trimming the seam allowances to remove excessive bulk that may prevent the collar from having sharp points at the edges or lying flat. Attach the collar to the blazer by matching points A on the collar to A on the blazer,

easing the collar into position to match the blazer edge to the open collar edge. Pin the collar securely in place and then stitch. The facings are now attached to the blazer fronts by placing them right sides together, sandwiching the collar between the facing and the blazer and aligning the front edges, before stitching in place.

5 The bottom edge of the blazer can now be hemmed but if you wish to add the bias binding, make sure the stitching is on the very edges to prevent it being visible when the blazer is completed. Place the blazer on the bear to check the sleeve length. Adjust, then pin the turned sleeve hems, remove the blazer and stitch securely in place. Attach the bias binding by starting with the sleeves. Unfold the binding and turn over about ½ inch (12mm) of the short edge to neaten. Pin the binding right sides together to the sleeve matching the edges and sew into place along the fold line. Fold the binding over the stitching and slip stitch to the inside of the sleeve. Finish the blazer in the same way. You will find it easier to use a separate length of binding for the collar.

6 Make a buttonhole now at the position indicated on the pattern and sew on the button. Finally a child's cap badge (obtainable from a school uniform supplier) is sewn into place for added realism.

7 To make the blouse, use the pattern for the pyjama top on pages 86–88. Cut out the pieces from white cotton fabric and then follow the instructions on page 84 for making the pyjama top. You may find it easier to omit the button holes and sew on a hook and loop fastening to the front edges of the blouse.

8 The skirt, a very simple pattern, is made by first cutting a rectangle of fabric 24 x 7 inches (60 x 18cm). Make a ½ inch (12mm) hem along one of the long edges, then along the remaining long edge, make a ¾ inch (20mm) casing for the elastic. Thread the elastic through the casing, securing it at the ends with sufficient stretch to give a suitable gather to the finished skirt. (Attach a closed safety pin to the elastic to help thread it through the casing.) Finally, fold the skirt in half, lining up the short edges and stitch together. The tie used here is a child's elasticated tie from a school uniform supplier, but one can be easily made from any suitable scrap of fabric.

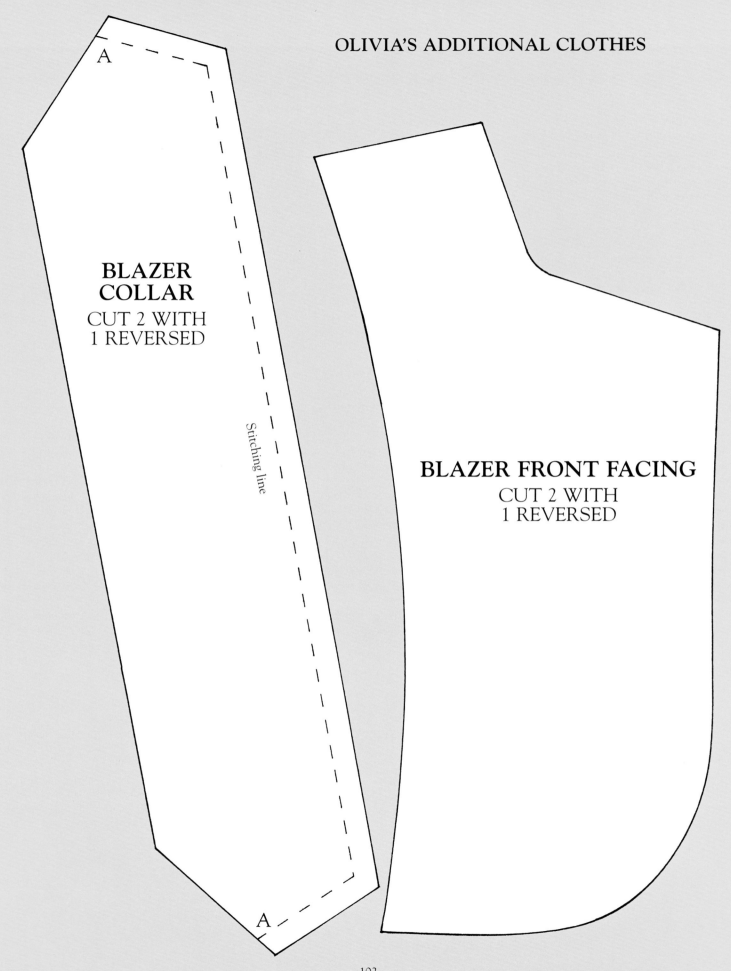

A

**BLAZER
COLLAR**
CUT 2 WITH
1 REVERSED

Stitching line

BLAZER FRONT FACING
CUT 2 WITH
1 REVERSED

A

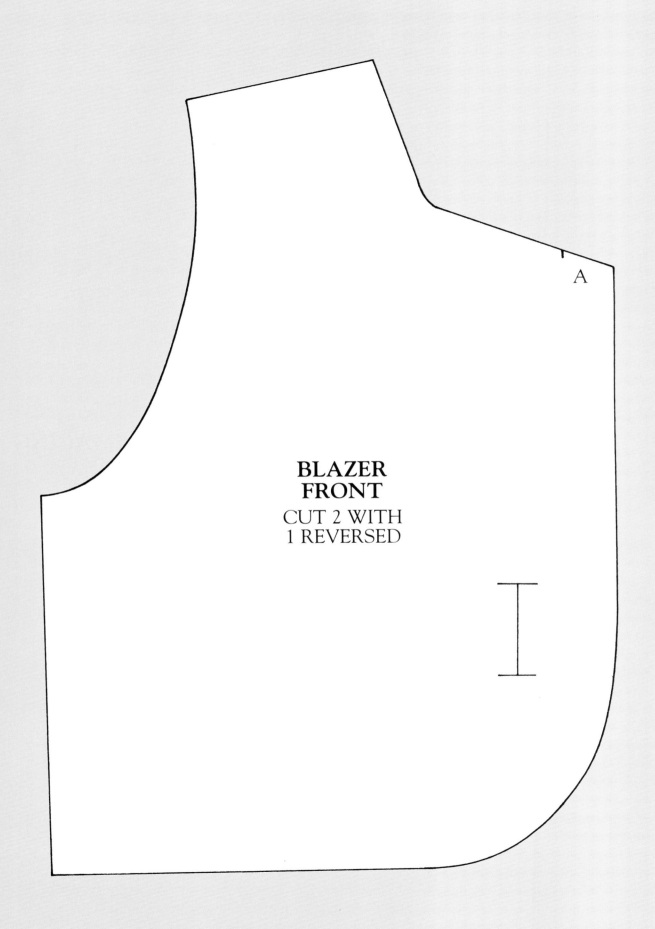

**BLAZER
FRONT**

CUT 2 WITH
1 REVERSED

A

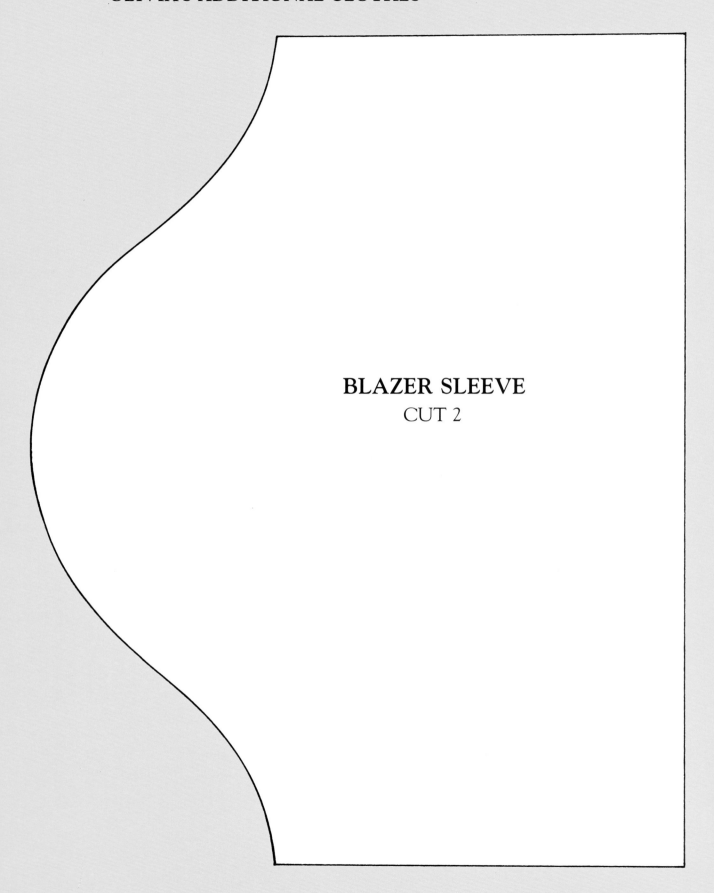

BLAZER SLEEVE
CUT 2

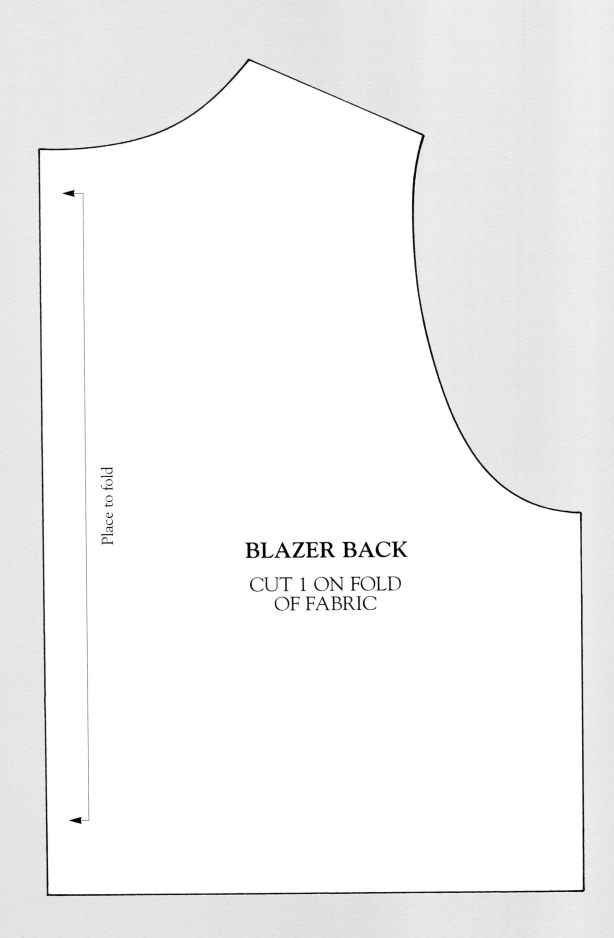

Place to fold

BLAZER BACK

CUT 1 ON FOLD
OF FABRIC

GRIZZLER

This 10 inch (260mm) teddy bear was inspired by a childhood memory of a visit to a zoo, of seeing grizzly bears sitting down looking upwards. Grizzler's arms have been designed to be long enough to cup his feet when he is sitting and also to allow him to be posed on all fours. There is a large traditional hump on his back and he is wood wool filled, with traditional glass eyes and leather paws and pads. We have used offcuts of clothing leather which, being soft and not too thick, is ideal for paws and pads. It is usually obtainable from craft shops in a variety of colours and shades.

MATERIALS

¼ yd (25cm) ½ inch (12mm) distressed pile mohair

2 x 1 inch (25mm) wooden joints for arms

3 x 1½ inch (36mm) wooden joints for legs and head

1 pair ¼ inch (7mm) black glass eyes

2 yd (1.8m) black nose thread

½ lb (250g) wood wool

2 oz (50g) polyester stuffing for paw areas

6 x 6 inches (150 x 150mm) soft leather or felt for pads

small piece black felt for nose template

1 reel sewing thread (to match fur fabric)

1 reel extra-strong thread (to match fur fabric)

1 Follow instructions on pages 20–21 for making pattern templates and cutting out the materials.

2 Grizzler's head, although appearing difficult, is not. The only real difference is that it is designed for the joint to be fitted at the back of the head rather than the base as normal. The head is still attached to the body in the usual way (see pages 28–29).

3 The making-up process is identical to all the other bears (see pages 20–33) except that Grizzler has leather paws and pads. These are attached in the same way as felt but you should use a spear point needle, size 90 (14), whether you are handsewing or using a machine. This needle has a three-sided point, shaped like a wedge, and will cut a slit in the leather rather than making a hole. This cut will close around the thread and grip it firmly.

4 Wood wool has been used for the stuffing, the method similar to polyester stuffing (see page 25) except that wood wool can sometimes be a little hard and be felt through softer material used for the pads. To prevent this and preserve the shape, fill the paws first with a small amount of polyester stuffing. Then fill up with wood wool, ensuring that any holes are firmly stuffed by frequent use of your stuffing stick and gently squeezing and moulding the filling as you go to achieve the final shape. On a small bear the wood wool may be a little long to fit easily into small areas such as arms and legs. If so, cut the wood wool into shorter, more manageable lengths.

5 After the bear is assembled and stuffed, the eyes and nose can be added in the normal way (see pages 31–33), clipping the muzzle back to suit your taste. Next the ears are attached (see page 30). Because of the head design the ears are fitted in a different position. Pin them into position quite a long way back on the head, using the photograph as a reference, and then sew them securely into place.

6 Finally groom the bear (see page 33) and finish off with a small leather collar if desired. If you wish, Grizzler can be stuffed entirely with polyester stuffing and given felt pads instead of leather – either way he will be a lovely bear.

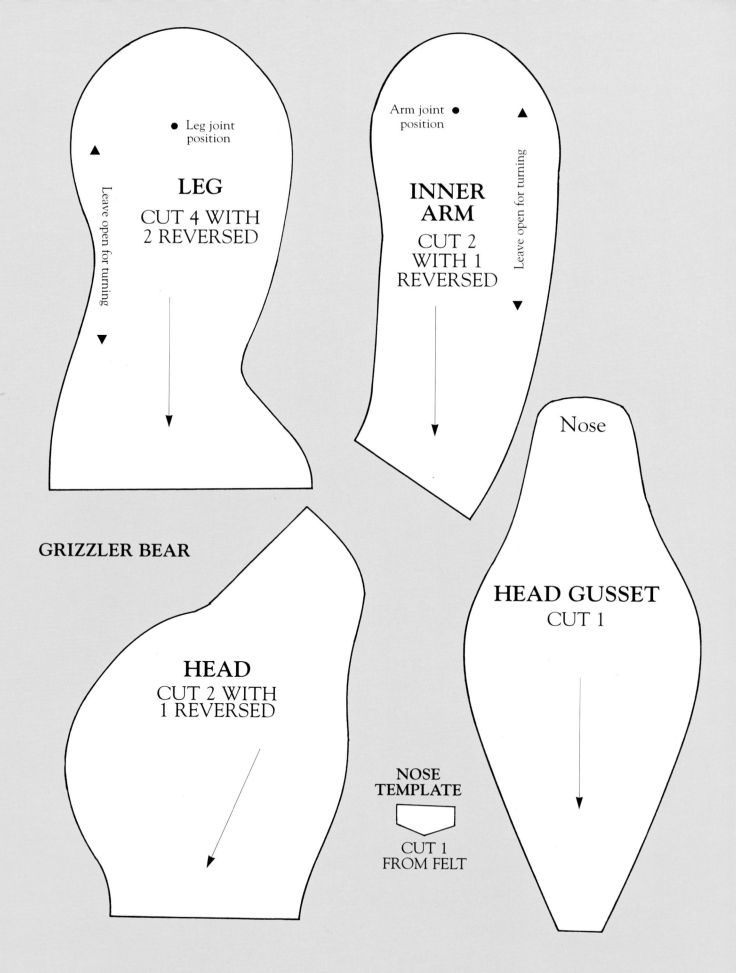

● Leg joint
position

LEG

**CUT 4 WITH
2 REVERSED**

Leave open for turning

Arm joint
position ●

**INNER
ARM**

**CUT 2
WITH 1
REVERSED**

Leave open for turning

Nose

HEAD GUSSET
CUT 1

GRIZZLER BEAR

HEAD

**CUT 2 WITH
1 REVERSED**

**NOSE
TEMPLATE**

CUT 1
FROM FELT

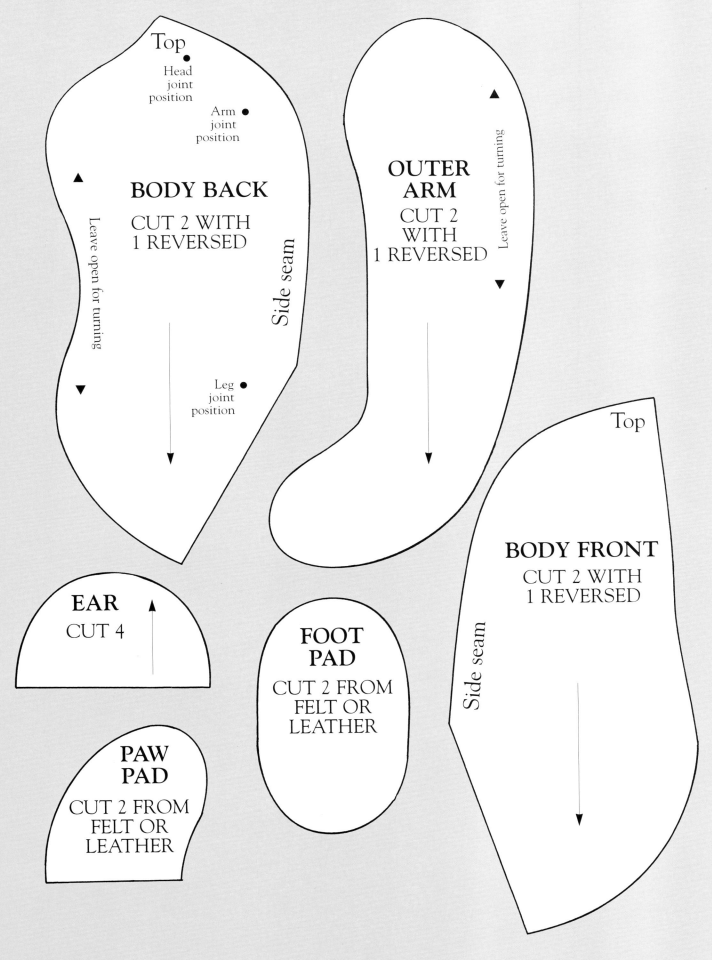

Top

Head
joint
position

Arm
joint
position

BODY BACK

**CUT 2 WITH
1 REVERSED**

Leave open for turning

Side seam

Leg
joint
position

**OUTER
ARM**

**CUT 2
WITH
1 REVERSED**

Leave open for turning

Top

BODY FRONT

**CUT 2 WITH
1 REVERSED**

Side seam

EAR

CUT 4

**FOOT
PAD**

**CUT 2 FROM
FELT OR
LEATHER**

**PAW
PAD**

**CUT 2 FROM
FELT OR
LEATHER**

MARMADUKE BEAR

This 20 inch (510mm) bear was inspired by the bears produced in the early part of this century by the German manufacturer Steiff. The centre seam on the head was devised as an economy measure to cope with the immense surge in demand for Steiff teddy bears between 1903 and 1908. The particular design Steiff used would yield six complete heads from the mohair material with enough left over for half a head, so in order to keep waste to the absolute minimum the centre seam which is now a much-sought-after feature on original collectors' bears was evolved. Also notable are the five claws embroidered on the pads and paws. This again was an early Steiff design which was used until 1905/6, after which the bears were given only four claws. Along with these features, we have incorporated the traditional humped back and long arms so characteristic of these early bears.

MATERIALS

24 x 54 inches (60 x 137cm) ½ inch (12mm) pile German embossed mohair
5 x 2 ½ inch (64mm) wooden joints
1 pair ½ inch (12mm) black glass eyes
5½ yd (5m) black nose thread
2½ lb (1 kg) polyester stuffing or equivalent
6 x 12 inches (15 x 30cm) wool felt for paws
small piece of black felt for nose template
1 reel sewing thread (to match fabric)
1 reel extra-strong thread (to match fabric)

1 Follow the instructions on pages 20–21 for making your pattern templates and cutting out the materials.

2 To make the head, take the two gusset pieces and pin the straight edges right sides together as shown in Fig.1, making sure that the edges are perfectly level and tucking in the pile between the fabric edges as you go. Take your time on this part as any unevenness or puckers will spoil the effect when the muzzle is clipped at the final stages.

3 Tack the edges together, remove the pins and then stitch along the length of the straight edge, starting at the nose (Fig.2). This will then give you the completed gusset to use when making the head in the normal way (see pages 24–25).

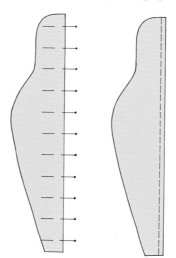

Fig.1 (far left) Pin the two head gusset pieces right sides together along the straight edge.

Fig.2 (left) Stitch securely in place along the straight edge, starting at the nose.

4 If you are using plastic safety eyes, fit these before stuffing the head (see page 38).

5 Next assemble the body, which is made of four pieces with the hump clearly defined on the

pattern. Whenever you are making a four-piece body design it is essential to identify the top and bottom of the pieces correctly and it is best to mark all four pieces clearly on the reverse of the fabric.

6 Marmaduke's arms are rather long, so after assembling the inner arm and pads (see pages 21–22) it is advisable to pin the outer and inner arm pieces together carefully. When you are completely satisfied that they are accurately aligned, tack in place to keep the pieces secure as the rather long pile used on this bear may cause them to move out of place while you are sewing. This small precaution will make the final stitching together a much simpler operation.

7 Next assemble the legs, following the instructions on pages 22–23.

8 Now assemble the bear in the usual way, starting by jointing the head to the body at the point shown on the pattern (see page 28). This positioning is important as it will allow the head to tilt slightly forward, avoiding a stark, upright look that would spoil the desired effect of this character.

9 Follow this by jointing the arms and legs (see page 29), ensuring that the placing of each limb is exact.

10 There is plenty of space for a growler in the body cavity of this bear, so if you decide to fit one follow one of the methods given on page 30 after the majority of the body has been stuffed (see page 30).

11 Close the back seam before moving on to the final finishing details. On many of the designs in this book the clipping of the muzzle is optional, but it really adds to the character and charm of this bear. Follow the instructions on page 33 and extend the clipping almost to the eyes as in the photograph.

12 Attach the ears in position with pins until you are happy with the look of your bear – you may find that they benefit from being slightly cupped to give a little depth. Sew both ears firmly in position and, if you are using glass eyes, attach them now (see pages 32–33).

13 To make the nose, glue the small black felt template in place and allow it to dry completely, then embroider over it with the nose thread (see page 31).

14 Embroider five claws on each paw and pad. To do this, simply thread a needle approximately 3 inches (75mm) long with a single thickness of your chosen nose thread, allowing roughly 20 inches (50cm) for each paw and pad. Attach the thread securely (see page 31) and follow Figs. 3–5, ensuring that the claws are sufficiently visible on the felt pads. If the material you are using has a longer pile than the one suggested, it may be advisable to trim the fur slightly with a pair of sharp scissors so that the stitched claws can be seen.

15 Finally, give Marmaduke a grooming with a teasel brush to free any pile trapped in the seams.

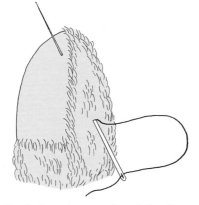

Fig.3 *Attach your thread firmly then bring the needle out at the first claw position on the felt pad.*

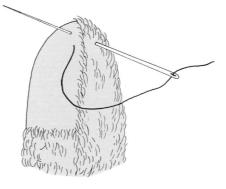

Fig.4 *Make one long stitch across the paw into the teddy's fur and bring the needle out at the second claw position.*

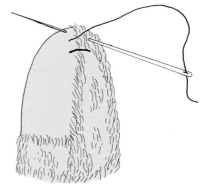

Fig.5 *Continue to make long stitches across the paw until the desired number of claws have been worked. Finish off the thread securely.*

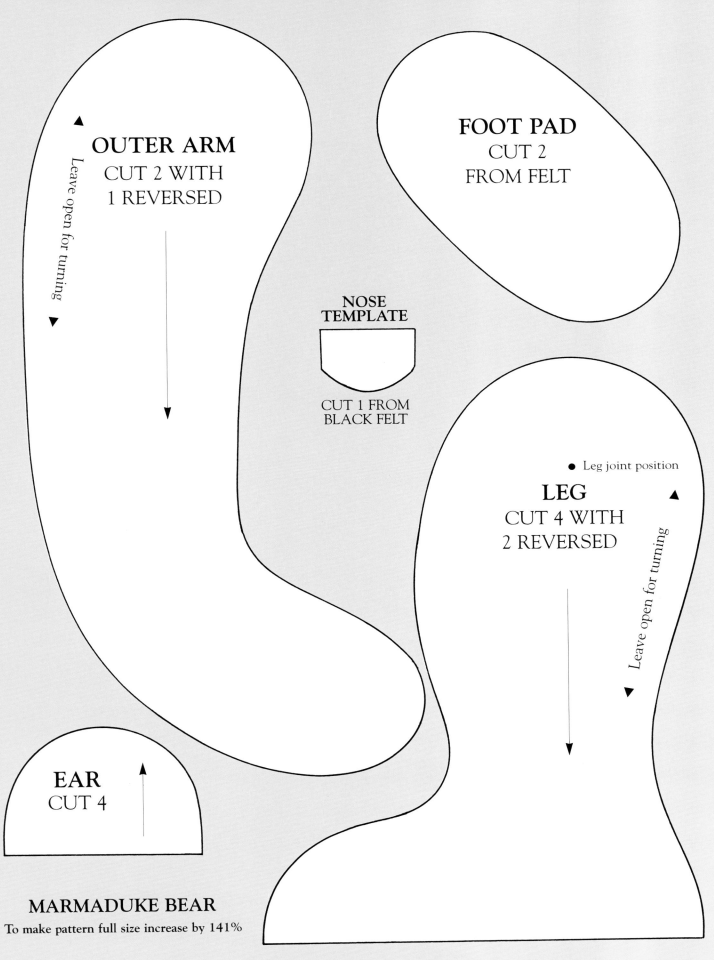

OUTER ARM
CUT 2 WITH
1 REVERSED

Leave open for turning

FOOT PAD
CUT 2
FROM FELT

NOSE TEMPLATE

CUT 1 FROM
BLACK FELT

● Leg joint position

LEG
CUT 4 WITH
2 REVERSED

Leave open for turning

EAR
CUT 4

MARMADUKE BEAR

To make pattern full size increase by 141%

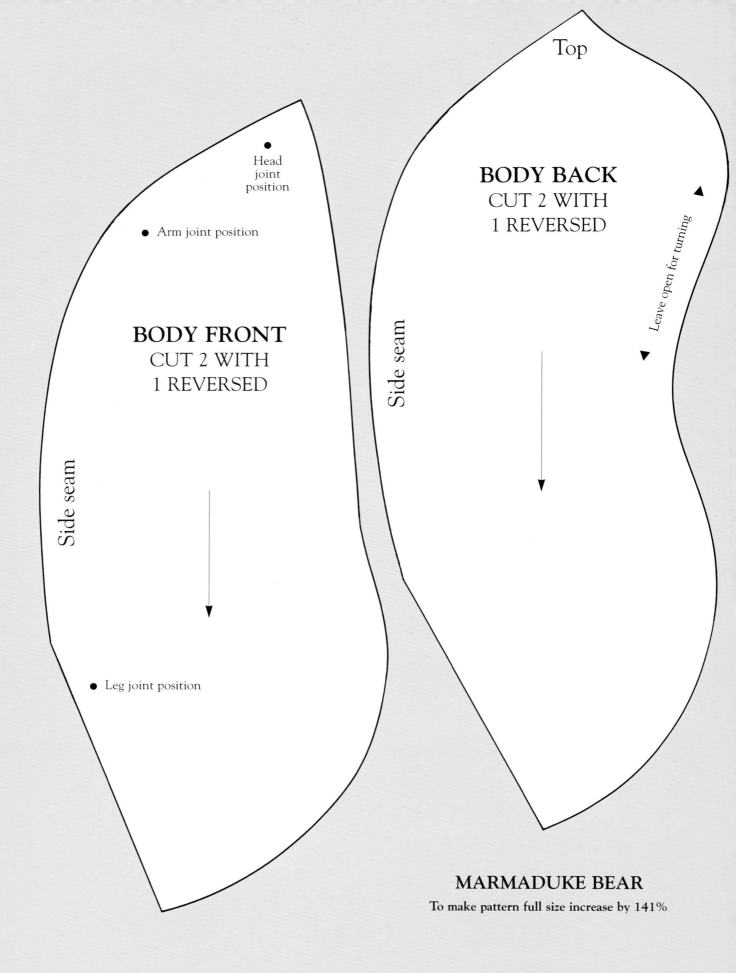

Head
joint
position

Arm joint position

BODY FRONT
CUT 2 WITH
1 REVERSED

Side seam

Leg joint position

Top

BODY BACK
CUT 2 WITH
1 REVERSED

Side seam

Leave open for turning

MARMADUKE BEAR

To make pattern full size increase by 141%

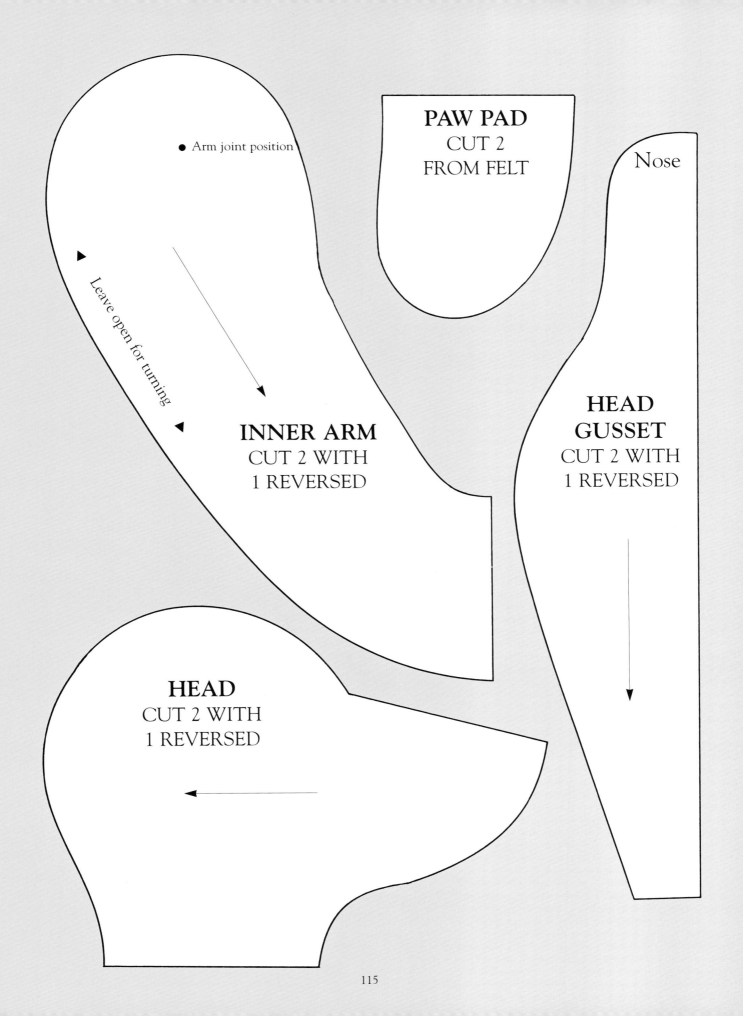

• Arm joint position

Leave open for turning

PAW PAD
CUT 2
FROM FELT

Nose

INNER ARM
CUT 2 WITH
1 REVERSED

**HEAD
GUSSET**
CUT 2 WITH
1 REVERSED

HEAD
CUT 2 WITH
1 REVERSED

HARVEY BEAR

Harvey is the largest teddy bear featured in this book, standing 30 inches (760mm) tall. He is made with tipped mohair, the two different colour tones giving a pleasing effect, and has the traditional teddy bear hump on his back. He is fitted with a double growler system and uses nut and bolt joints throughout. As you can see from the photographs, he is certainly an impressive teddy bear and he would make an excellent addition to any collection of traditional teddy bears. However, he could equally well be made from a synthetic fur fabric and be fitted with plastic safety eyes and joints if you wish to make him as a present for a child.

MATERIALS

1 yd (91cm) of 1 inch (25mm) pile tipped mohair

5 x 3 inch (75mm) wooden joints with nut and bolt fixings

1 pair ¾ inch (18mm) amber glass eyes

5½ yd (5m) black nose thread

3lb (1250g) polyester stuffing

12 x 12 inches (300 x 300mm) wool mix felt for pads

small piece black felt for nose template

1 reel sewing thread (to match fur fabric)

1 reel extra-strong thread (to match fur fabric)

2 growlers (optional)

1 Follow instructions on pages 20–21 for making pattern templates and cutting out the materials.

2 This bear uses the double head gusset as featured on Marmaduke bear – for instructions, see page 110.

If you are using plastic safety eyes, remember to fit them before stuffing the head (see page 38).

3 When the bear is sewn and turned (see pages 20–25) he is ready for jointing. As the arms and legs on a bear of this size are comparatively heavy, nut and bolt fixings have been used as they will give added strength and stiffness to the joints. These joints are assembled and fitted exactly as you would a normal split pin joint (see pages 25–29) except that the split pin is replaced by a bolt of sufficient length to enable the final washer and nut to be added from inside the body. It is easiest to use a standard nut rather than a nyloc one. When the head or limb is in place with the bolt protruding into the body cavity, place a flat washer on the bolt followed by a nut of the correct size and tighten so that the head or limb can be moved easily with just a little resistance. When you are satisfied, secure the nut in place by adding a second nut to the bolt (this time with no washer) and then, holding the first nut with a spanner, tighten the second nut against the first with another spanner. This will lock the nut so securely that it can only be dismantled again with spanners.

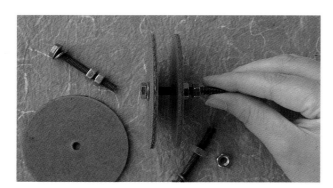

A nut and bolt joint.

Tightening a nut and bolt joint.

4 The double growler system, first used in the early part of the century, permits the teddy bear to growl when he is tipped either forwards or backwards. Place the two growlers beside each other, with one growler reversed so the holes will be at the opposite end to the other growler. Tape the two growlers together firmly, using either strong carpet tape or parcel tape, and install them horizontally into the body cavity of the bear (see page 30).

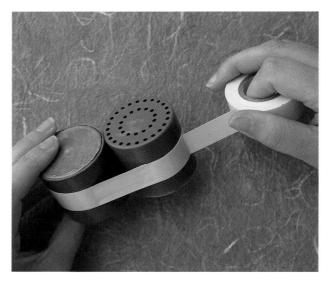

The double growler system.

5 Finally, the muzzle. If you are using a tipped mohair, remember that as you clip it at the muzzle the base shade of colouring will become more pronounced so a little caution is advisable.

Clipping the muzzle.

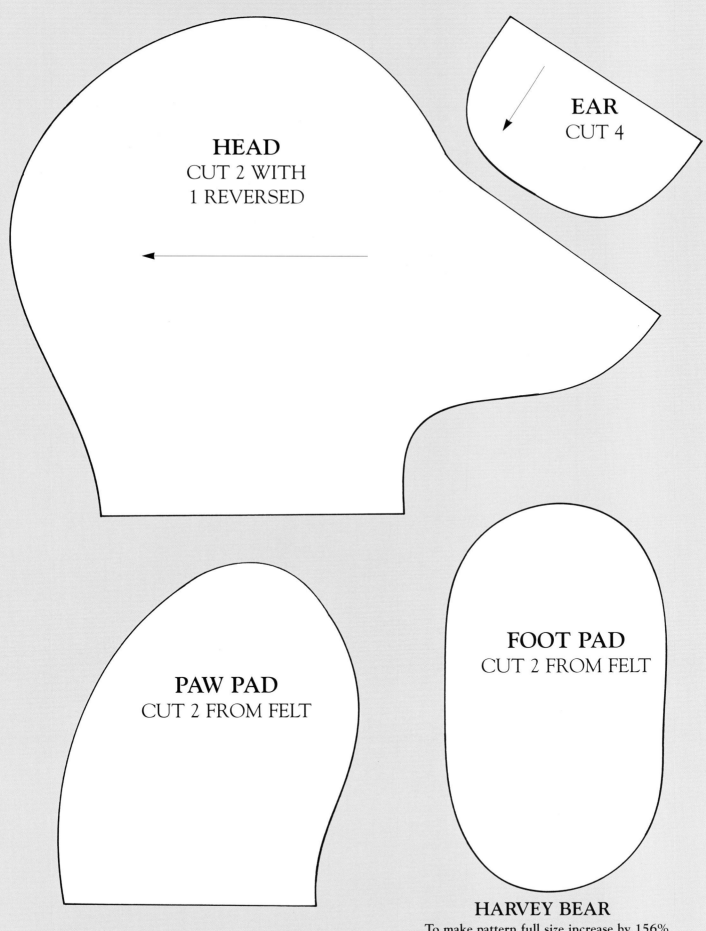

HEAD
CUT 2 WITH
1 REVERSED

EAR
CUT 4

PAW PAD
CUT 2 FROM FELT

FOOT PAD
CUT 2 FROM FELT

HARVEY BEAR
To make pattern full size increase by 156%

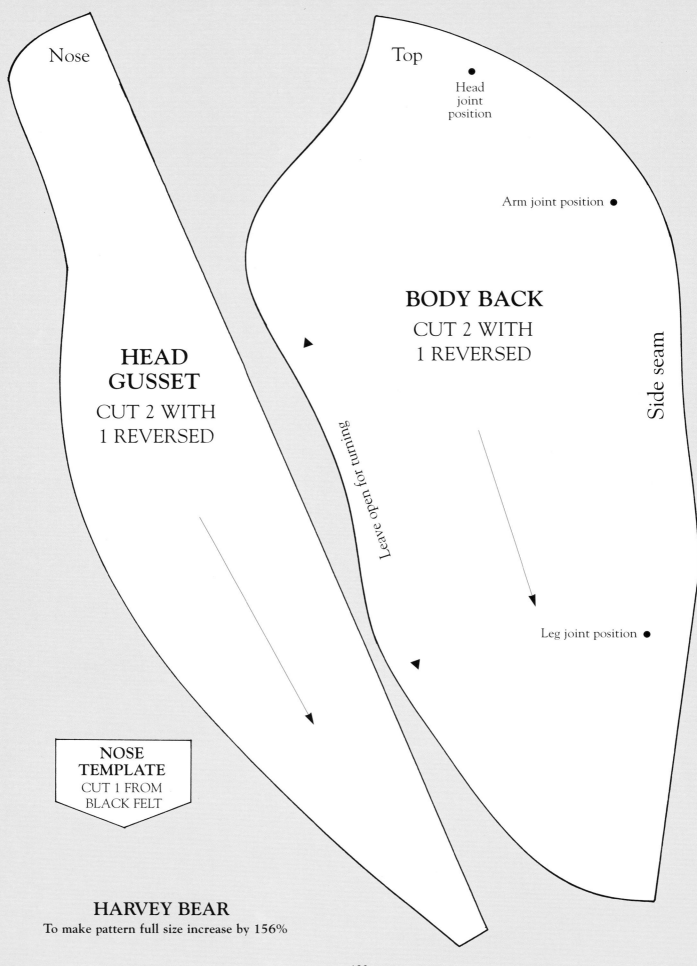

Nose

Top

Head
joint
position

Arm joint position ●

**HEAD
GUSSET**

CUT 2 WITH
1 REVERSED

BODY BACK

CUT 2 WITH
1 REVERSED

Side seam

Leave open for turning

Leg joint position ●

**NOSE
TEMPLATE**
CUT 1 FROM
BLACK FELT

HARVEY BEAR
To make pattern full size increase by 156%

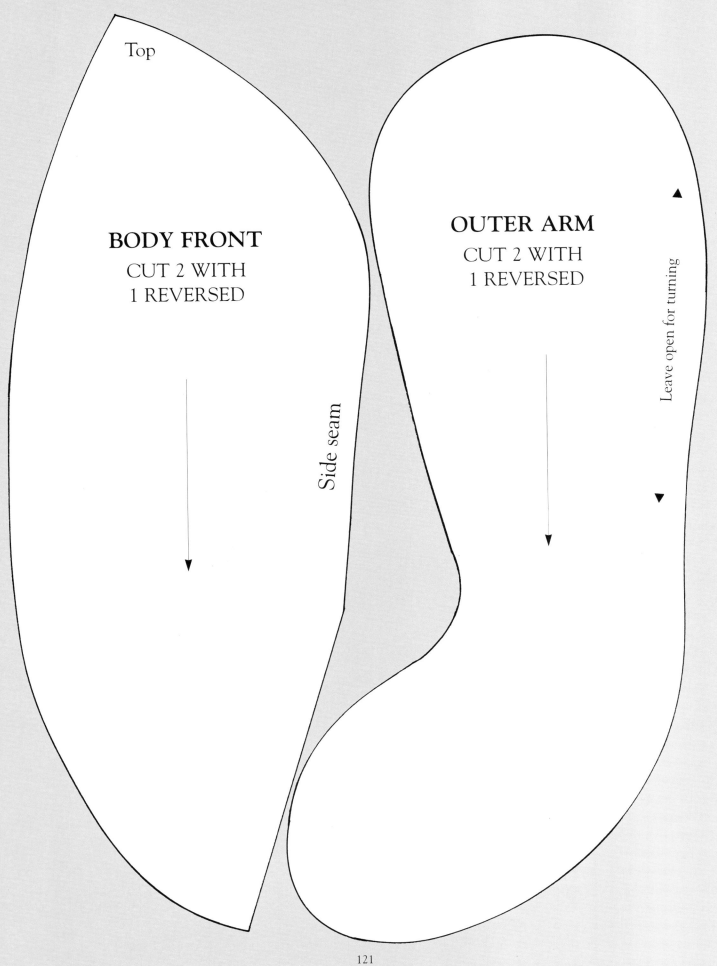

Top

BODY FRONT

CUT 2 WITH
1 REVERSED

Side seam

OUTER ARM

CUT 2 WITH
1 REVERSED

Leave open for turning

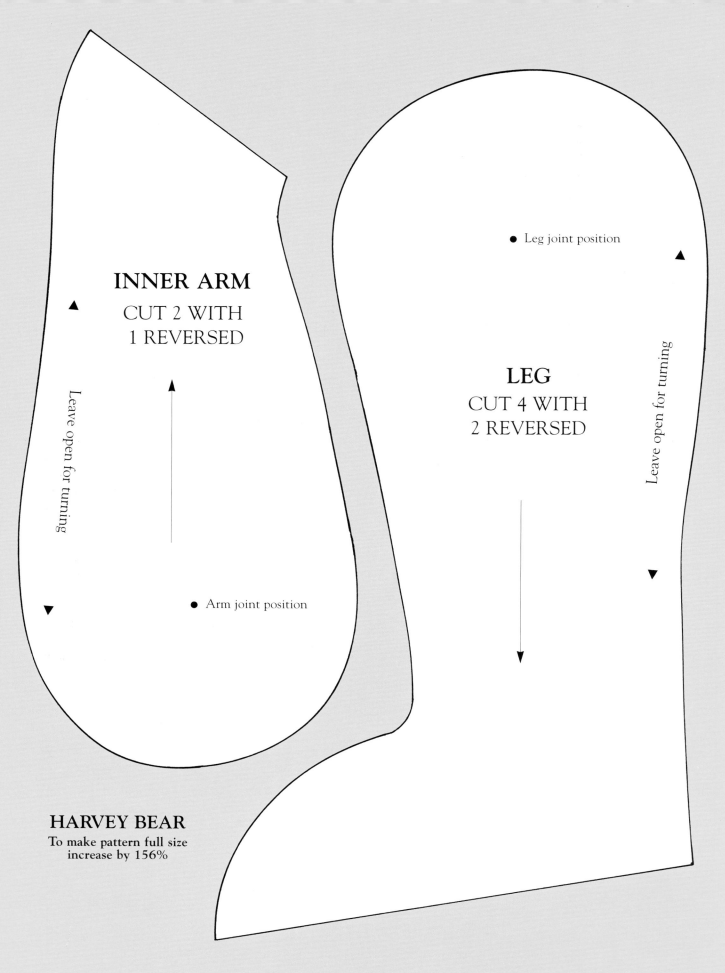

INNER ARM
CUT 2 WITH
1 REVERSED

Leave open for turning

Arm joint position

● Leg joint position

LEG
CUT 4 WITH
2 REVERSED

Leave open for turning

HARVEY BEAR
To make pattern full size
increase by 156%

THE RESTORATION OF TEDDY BEARS

This chapter will take you through a few techniques to restore an old teddy bear to his former glory. First of all, it must be emphasized that you should only attempt to do restoration work on an old teddy bear if it is not very valuable: if your bear is 40 years old or more the chances are that it could well be worth something, so it is strongly recommended that you first seek expert valuation. If your bear is of value or you simply do not feel confident enough to do your own restoration, you should employ one of the many professional teddy bear restorers who can be contacted through the specialist publications listed at the back of the book. Alternatively, you will probably be able to find someone through recommendation from one of the teddy bear museum curators. However, before entrusting a valuable teddy to any restorer, do make absolutely sure that the person who is to carry out this work for you is suitably qualified and competent.

If you decide to proceed, you should restrict your repairs to those which are absolutely necessary so that you do not detract from the original character of your teddy bear. The first step is to assess the amount of damage that the bear has sustained; the usual problems are broken joints, missing eyes and ears and an overall layer of dirt. The following steps outline the most common procedures involved in restoring a bear. Before starting any repair you should read through this section thoroughly as some of the techniques interrelate, such as fitting a replacement paw pad, for example – this operation can be done at the same time as replacing a joint where the bear is already dismantled.

SURFACE CLEANING

If the teddy bear is generally in quite good condition, the only course of action needed will simply be surface cleaning. To do this, first use a soft brush to remove any surface dust and dirt and then vacuum the entire surface of the bear thoroughly, covering the nozzle of the vacuum cleaner with an open-weave cotton or muslin cloth to reduce the power of the suction and also prevent the possibility of losing an eye or similar from the teddy into the vacuum cleaner.

Next, fill a bowl with clean, warm (not hot) water and add enough mild, unscented baby shampoo to produce a generous amount of white foam. The foam is the cleaning agent and therefore it is the foam only that is applied to the teddy bear, not the water. Apply it generously with a wad of white cotton material such as a clean handkerchief so that you can assess the amount of dirt being removed and there will not be any risk of dye from your cleaning cloth being transferred to the bear.

Rub the cloth lightly in small circular movements to work the foam into the pile of the fur, covering small areas of the bear at a time – do not try to clean the entire bear in one operation as it is far better and easier to work slowly and methodically at this stage. From the amount of dirt that appears on your cloth you will be able to see how quickly the dirt is removed and decide how many applications will be necessary to completely clean this particular part of the bear.

Repeat the process with several clean cloths until the cloth remains clean, then rinse the surface of the bear with clean, warm water using another clean cotton or towelling cloth and towel dry to remove as much moisture as possible. The bear is best left to dry naturally in an airing cupboard, but you can use a hairdryer set to the coolest temperature and the slowest speed. When absolutely dry, lightly brush the fur with a soft brush to lift the pile. If the cleaning has been done properly, no wetness will have penetrated the outer skin. This is vitally important, as any wooden or card joints, wood wool or kapok stuffing and of course any metal components will suffer from contact with water.

REPLACING A LOST EYE

Very often a teddy bear will have lost one or both of his eyes, and these may have been replaced with unsuitable substitutes – even trouser buttons! To restore the sight of your teddy bear, the first step is to try to identify what the original bear looked like. This is relatively easy, as there are quite a few reference books on the subject of old teddy bears that you can refer to. If you cannot find your particular bear, you will have to make a decision as to what eyes would suit him (unless of course there is an original eye remaining). Having obtained replacements, the first step is to remove any 'modern' substitutes. If you look closely at the eye sockets you will often see the point of attachment of the original eyes, perhaps as tell-tale signs of a small rust mark on the fur caused by the wire shanks. If no clues are apparent on your particular bear and there are no photographic references in books to guide you, the siting of the replacement eyes will be a matter of judgement and of following the instructions on pages 32–33.

REPLACING A LOST EAR

A common sight on old teddy bears is the lost ear syndrome, usually caused by generations of children picking up the bear by the ears. The easiest way to replace an ear is to make a replica, using the remaining ear as a pattern. Remove the ear from the bear carefully, making a note or sketch of the original position, then unpick it and open it out fully to reveal the two original fabric shapes. Make a tracing of these shapes and then cut out duplicates from new fur, trying as far as possible to ensure the new ear pieces are in a matching fabric. It will be virtually impossible to obtain a perfect match, so take one piece of the original ear and sew it to a replacement ear piece. Repeat for the other ear and you will now have two matching ears. Sew one of the new hybrid ears back on to the head where the ear that you removed earlier was sited, with the new fur piece at the back. Then, using the first ear as a reference point, position the second ear, secure it with pins and when you are happy they are both equally spaced, sew it permanently into place.

REPLACING LOST OR BROKEN JOINTS

Apart from the ears, the other point of strain on teddy bears is one of the limbs, often an arm, that eventually becomes detached or very loose. Using a loose arm as an example, the first step is to open the body cavity to investigate the cause of the problem. To do this, you first have to open the final closing seam that the manufacturer would have sewn by hand. This is usually found on the back of the bear, and is generally quite easy to locate as the stitching is often a little heavier and larger. Open the seam with the points of sharp scissors, making sure that when snipping the threads you do not inadvertently cut any of the fabric. Remove the threads and then the stuffing to reveal the offending joint. If it is generally in good condition, it will simply be a matter of tightening the joint in the manner described on page 29. However, early bears often had card joints and these can disintegrate over the years, or it may be that the cotter or split pin has rusted through or broken, in which case the whole joint has to be replaced. If this is the case, the arm will need to be removed from the body completely by straightening the legs of the split pin or in severe cases cutting or sawing through the metal pin. After this, the arm is opened and the stuffing removed exactly as described for the body in order to remove the old joint. Use a replacement joint of the correct size and fit as described on page 27. A decision has to be made at this stage as to whether the other joints should be replaced; the golden rule is to replace any parts only where absolutely necessary in order to preserve the originality of the teddy bear as far as possible.

PAW PADS

If one or other of the pads needs replacing, this is best accomplished by first identifying what material the original pads were made from. Ideally the replacement material should be as close a match as possible, both in fabric and of course colour. Next make a paper template slightly larger than the original pad, then, using this template, cut out the replacement pad from the new material. Fold under the excess material to match the outline of the original pad, tack in place on top of the original and then oversew the pad into place using very small neat stitches. If you prefer to replace the original pad entirely, you will have to unpick the whole arm and fit a complete new pad as described on page 21.

STUFFING

The bear may be complete and undamaged apart from the stuffing, or lack of it. Over the years wood wool teddy bears often suffer the collapse of their stuffing, often into piles of dust that gather at the extremities of the limbs and body, leaving the rest of the bear empty and lifeless. Where possible, the bear should be refilled with the same material as used in the original and in the case of wood wool this is often only available from specialist teddy bear suppliers. If you do have any difficulties the alternatives are polyester or kapok. Remove all traces of old stuffing and discard it if unusable, then make sure that the bear is free of dust and bugs. If any of the latter are found, place the bear inside a plastic bag along with mothballs or flea powder, seal the bag and leave it for 24 hours. Vacuum out the entire skin thoroughly and then simply restuff following the instructions on page 29–30.

NOSES AND PAWS

The last remaining item that may require attention is the embroidering of the nose and paw pads. With noses, the original threads must be removed if they are beyond salvation and the nose restitched following the outline of the original stitching – if you look closely, you should be able to see the original needle holes quite easily. The paws and claws are treated in exactly the same manner.

MUSEUMS AND COLLECTIONS

Margarete Steiff Museum,
Giengen (Brenz),
Germany.

The Bournemouth Bears,
Expocentre,
Old Christchurch Lane,
Bournemouth,
BH1 1NE.
Tel 01202 293544.

Broadway Bears Museum,
76 High Street,
Broadway,
Worcestershire,
WR12 7AJ.
Tel/Fax 01386 858323.

The Bear Museum,
38 Dragon Street,
Petersfield,
Hampshire,
GU31 4JJ.
Tel 01730 265108.

Scotland's Teddy Bear Museum,
The Wynd,
Melrose,
Scotland,
TD6 9LB.
Tel 01896 822464.

The Teddy Bear Museum,
19 Greenhill Street,
Stratford-upon-Avon,
Warwickshire,
CV37 6LF.
Tel 01789 293160.

Bethnal Green Museum of Childhood,
Cambridge Heath Road,
London,
E2 9PA.
Tel 0181 9811711.

USEFUL ADDRESSES

Note: it is wise to check with suppliers by phone to see if any charge is made for catalogues or samples.

Fluffy's Teddy Bear Warehouse,
Unit 11, D2 Trading Estate,
Castle Road, Sittingbourne,
Kent,
ME10 3RH.
Tel 01795 478775.
Suppliers of German and English mohair fabric and bear-making accessories.

Ancestral Collectors Bears,
Avon House, Suite 29A New Broad Street,
Old Town, Stratford-upon-Avon,
Warwickshire,
CV37 6HW.
Tel/Fax 01789 268348.
Suppliers of English and German mohair and bear-making accessories.

Lyrical Bears,
P.O. Box 111, Welwyn Garden City,
Hertfordshire,
AL6 0XT.
Tel 01438 351651.
Suppliers of miniature bear-making fabrics and accessories.

Oakley Fabrics Ltd,
8 May Street, Luton,
Bedfordshire,
LU1 3QY.
Tel 01582 424828/34733.
Fax 01582 455274.
Suppliers of a large range of mohair and synthetic fur fabrics and bear and toy-making accessories.

A. Helmbold GmbH. Plüschweberei und Fäberei
D-98634 Oberweid,
Haupstrasse 44,
Germany.
Tel/Fax Germany 036946-22009.
Manufacturers of toy plush made from mohair, wool, alpaca, cotton and artificial silk.

Bridon Bears,
'Bears Cottage',
42 St Michaels Lane,
Bridport,
Dorset,
DT6 3RD.
Tel/Fax 01308 420796.
Net address http://freespace.virgin.net/bridon.bears
Manufacturers of traditional collector's bears, trade enquiries invited. Also suppliers of English mohair, bear-making accessories and a large pattern range.

Bumbles Antiques and Collectables,
Jean Rawlinson,
13 Princes Crescent,
Hove,
East Sussex,
BN3 4GS.
Tel 01273 239755.
New and antique teddy bear sales, also teddy bear restoration service.

Edinburgh Imports Inc.,
POB 722-Woodland Hills,
California 91365-0722
U.S.A.
Tel 818 591-3800.
Fax 818 591-3806.
Suppliers of teddy bear components with an extensive range of mohair fabric.

Nonsuch Fabrics,
The Gables,
King Edward Road,
Axminster,
Devon,
EX13 5PP.
Tel 01297 35017.
Fax 01297 35457.
Suppliers of a good range of fine English and German mohairs, a good selection of pile lengths and finishes.

FURTHER READING

The following publications contain a wealth of information and useful addresses.

Teddy Bear Times,
Avalon Court, Star Road, Partridge Green,
West Sussex,
RH13 8RY.
Tel 01403 711511. Fax 01403 711521.
Teddy-bear fair organizers and publishers of monthly teddy bear magazine for enthusiasts and collectors. Also from this publisher, *Bear Collector,* a quarterly magazine available via subscription.

The Teddy Bear Club International Magazine,
Castle House,
97 High Street,
Colchester,
Essex,
CO1 1TH.
Tel 01206 540621.
One of Britain's most popular teddy bear magazines featuring bear patterns, top tips and in depth features every month. With hundreds of give aways and prizes as well, this is a must for all arctophiles.

The UK Teddy Bear Guide,
P.O. Box 290, Brighton,
East Sussex,
BN2 1DR.
Tel 01273 697974. Fax 01273 626255.
An annual publication containing comprehensive listings of the British teddy bear world, including details of material suppliers, teddy bear artists, shops, fairs, shows and events. Organizers of the British Teddy Bear Association (BTBA) for up-to-date news, special offers and bear contacts. Worldwide membership available.

Teddy Bear Scene (*& Other Furry Friends*),
7 Ferringham Lane, Ferring,
West Sussex,
BN12 5ND.
Tel 01903 244900. Fax 01903 506626.
This bi-monthly publication covers all aspects of the hobby from the beginner to the most avid of arctophiles.

ACKNOWLEDGEMENTS

The authors would like to thank the following for their help and generosity with materials and assistance during the writing of this book.

Dave Wilkinson of Fluffy Fabrics for providing materials for Edwin, Haydn and Marmaduke bears.

Elizabeth Meredith of Ancestral Collectors Bears for providing the material used for Jasper and Alonzo, and for joints and glass eyes.

Christopher Pointeer of Lyrical Bears for materials for Smudge and the miniature bear-making tools.

Roy Pilkington of Oakley Fabrics for his contribution towards material used for Harvey and Bertie and for wool felt.

Barbara Ann Bears for providing the majority of the glass eyes used throughout.

The mohair fabric used for Grizzler, Barnaby, Oliver and Olivia is from the Bridon Bear range and is available via mail order.

Jean Rawlinson of 'Bumbles', Cheltenham, for the loan of the antique teddy bears photographed in this book.

Finally our grateful thanks to all the team at David and Charles publishers who have made this book possible.

INDEX

Numbers in *italic* indicate illustrations